Instructions for using AR

LET AUGMENTED REALITY CHANGE HOW YOU READ A BOOK

With your smartphone, iPad or tablet you can use the **Hasmark AR** app to invoke the augmented reality experience to literally read outside the book.

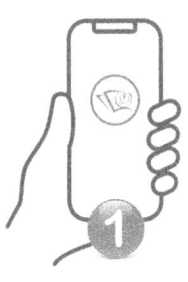
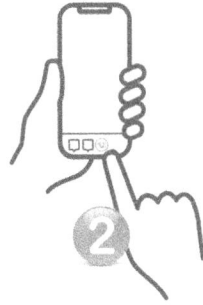
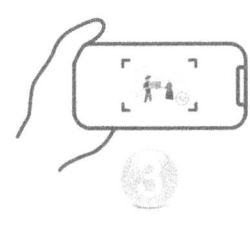

1. Download the **Hasmark app** from the **Apple App Store** or **Google Play**

2. Open and select the option

3. Point your lens at the full image with the and enjoy the augmented reality experience.

Go ahead and try it right now with the cover of this book.

Once the content begins, click the '**Lock**' icon to lock the content onto your phone.

REACH PEAK FUNCTIONING IN
ONE MONTH OR 21 STEPS

TRAIN
YOUR OWN
HERO

DON GREENE, PH.D.

Endorsements

"Musicians face an intensely competitive orchestral job market and the reality that a three-minute audition can determine a lifelong career. Dr. Greene…gives young musicians a concrete set of skills to achieve the concentrated focus needed in these critical moments. The response of our musicians has been immediate and we often hear what a difference it has made in their concert performances, as well as their experience of the audition process."

Michael Tilson Thomas
Artistic Director, New World Symphony Academy
Music Director and Conductor, San Francisco Symphony

"I highly recommend Don Greene's book about creating successful performances at the highest levels of functioning in a variety of pursuits. He has cracked the code about why talented people make unforced errors and unnecessary mistakes, which happen too often at the worst possible times. Then he trains them how to achieve their best, especially under competitive pressure or creative deadlines. This amazing book is packed full of inspiring stories about people's struggles in a number of different but challenging endeavors. I consider *Train Your Own Hero* a must read for all performers, competitive athletes and creative artists."

Kathy Rose
International Best-Selling Author
Claiming Your Voice

"How do you know what you don't know if you don't know that you know it?" In this book, Dr. Greene has put all the illuminating information and practical concepts together in a clear and comprehensible way. He will train you how to focus intensely and exclusively on the task at hand in the continuing moment of now. Follow his lead and do what he recommends and you will be able to access your highest levels of functioning when it really counts."

Luke Guldan
Producer, director, actor
NBC's Emmy Nominated series, *The Good Place*
CBS's show, *Tell Me A Story* The Guldan Ratio.com

"Dr. Greene prepared me to do the work necessary to dance at the top level in competition and win. When I stepped on the dance floor, I set my posture correctly, lifted my chin, and said to myself, 'I am the World Champion. I am going to show everyone all that I know and triumph'. In my mind, there was no other possibility. There was no negativity, fear or doubt. I Centered myself in the here and released all the tension from my body. I danced as if I'd already won and then I did."

Pamela R.
Former Opera Singer
7 Time World Ballroom Dancing Champion

"Dr. Don Greene has helped me accomplish my full potential as a visual artist and graphic designer. His amazing tools enhanced my focus in the studio and helped me build gallery representation and patron relationships. His invaluable Centering strategy has given me a reliable way to achieve a highly creative mindset before I ever set foot in my studio. With his guidance, I'm able to project the confidence needed for me to grow as an artist. I recognize with gratitude the gifts I possess and the opportunities yet to come."

Richard Lang Chandler, painter
https://www.richardlangchandler.com/

I was fortunate to work closely with Sports Psychologist Don Greene for many years, both off and on the pool deck. He came to our practices frequently, counseled our divers away from the pool, taught them valuable skills and strategies, attended team meetings, and travelled with us to the National Championships, Olympic Trials, Olympic Games, World Championships and World Cup. He was a major factor in the success of our athletes in national and international competitions.

Dr. Ron O'Brien, Ed.D.
8 Time US Olympic Diving Coach
12 Olympic medals with 5 gold
13 World Championship and World Cup gold medals

"Other than my coach, Ron O'Brien, no one but Dr. Don Greene knows how I repeatedly created peak performances at the highest level of competition in challenging circumstances. He will bring you to a greater understanding and consciousness about performing at your best when it really counts. The key concepts that helped me were visualization, creative and free expression, and the love of my coach and his guidance."

Greg Louganis
Olympic Diver
Actor, Dancer, Author

"In the late '90's, we were struggling as a department and firm. We needed a different model, a new way of thinking. I found another kind of consultant, a sports psychologist. I wanted someone who could elevate my senior traders' performance to a higher level. As a golfer who usually shot in the mid-80's, I also wanted a professional who could help me break 80. As a result of his guidance, my team's P&L went up 21%. Since then, I shot a 75 at a championship golf course and broke 80 more than 30 times."

Edward McMahon
Former Managing Director of Trading, Merrill Lynch
Former Senior Vice-President, New York Stock Exchange

TRAIN YOUR OWN HERO

*Reach Peak Functioning
in One Month or 21 Steps*

DON GREENE, Ph.D.

Hasmark Publishing
www.hasmarkpublishing.com

Editors: Erin S. Armstrong, MFA, https://LeewardShores.com
Emily R. Mace, Ph.D., https://emilyrmace.com

Alison Malcolm, ali@hasmarkpublishing.com
Cover: Alan Dino Hebeland Ian Koviak, www.bookdesigners.com
Book Design: Amit Dey amit@hasmarkpublishing.com

ISBN 13: 978-1-77482-119-0
ISBN 10: 1774821192

Dedication

I dedicate this work to my dearest and most valued friends: Kathy Rose, Eddie McMahon, Ron and Mary Jane O'Brien, Chris and Beth McLachlin, Barbara and Richard Chandler, Annie Bosler and Dylan Hart. Thank you for your friendship and love.

Foreword

$\mathcal{E}$very coach, teacher, and mentor wants their charge to be as good as they possibly can be and to realize their full potential. For the individual, hopefully their desire is to become great, perhaps even famous. They want to get as close as possible to their highest level of performance under pressure, when it really counts. The question is *how*?

Many athletes and performers have become great because they have figured out what it takes. Maybe they stumbled onto a formula that usually works for them, but it doesn't work consistently, and their performance is erratic. Other people find a technique or method that helps them temporarily, but they have to look for a new rabbit's foot for each challenge.

Performance is 95% an act of physical expression, either through fine motor or gross motor activity. The other 5% is found in the mind, which controls that 95%. So, although the physical skills may be highly developed and superb, they depend on the mind to achieve the peak level of one's true capabilities. How can this crucial 5% of performance be developed and mastered?

Dr. Don Greene has created this outstanding guide and instructional manual to prepare individuals for the very best performances of their lives. It can be used for any type of sports competition, the performing arts, or public speaking. It works for any activity dealing with a person's desire to do their absolute best under high stress when it matters the most.

Dr. Greene has coached many athletes to win Olympic gold medals, world swimming titles, PGA and LPGA Tournaments, and Grand Prix championships. He has trained opera singers, musicians, ballet dancers, and actors to win professional auditions. He has taught senior traders and brokers on Wall Street how to raise their P&L (bottom line) by 21%

Train Your Own Hero is organized day by day, step by step, leading the reader to the mastery of peak performance skills. Dr. Greene starts the process at the base level of what you need to know, outlining exactly what you need to do in order to achieve your highest goals. Understand now that to reach your physical performance goals, these critical mental skills must be learned and practiced repeatedly over time.

As you will see, Dr. Greene has created an intense and comprehensive program for attaining high levels of performance in challenging endeavors. It is set up as a crash course, if needed, to be completed in as little as four weeks. If you have more time, the process can be extended by a month or two. Either way, be assured that it works! You will be surprised and pleased with the outcome. This is the only program I know of that provides a highly sophisticated and proven approach to train all the components of peak functioning.

Dr. R. Craig Poole, Ed.D. Head Coach,
US Olympic Training Center, Track and Field 2010–2014

Introduction

*W*elcome! This is a high-powered, intensive, performance-oriented program designed to help you achieve a peak level of functioning in 21 steps or about four weeks. This proven approach can be effectively applied to any challenging activity in which you already have an intermediate or advanced level of proficiency. You just need a journal, notebook, and the desire to take your performance to a much higher level at a real event. The event could be a music performance, audition, dance competition, academic test, speech, creative project, or athletic contest, like a golf game or tennis match.

The goal is for you to reach a peak level of functioning in about four weeks. The program is arranged to start on a Monday with step 1. I will then take you day by day for the next four weeks, or through the 21 steps, and offer everything that I know to get you ready for a flawless performance.

I'm very excited to share a true hero's journey with you. Greg Louganis is a former Olympic champion diver and truly amazing person. As you'll see, he struggled through many years of terrible treatment and horrible circumstances, and he courageously made it through to the other side. More so than anyone I've met, Greg Louganis knows about peak functioning under extreme pressure.

I will also offer you the incredible wisdom of Ron O'Brien, who was Greg's diving coach. Ron was a former collegiate diver on both the 3-meter springboard and 10-meter platform. He went on to become an eight-time Olympic diving coach and he trained every US Olympic team from 1968 to 1996. In my professional opinion, he's one of the world's best athletic coaches, but I am biased because he's also one of my closest friends.

After our glory days and years training Olympic athletes, Ron and I stayed in touch. Not long ago, Ron told me about a short article he'd written about success and peak performance. The piece was entitled, "Success Doesn't Just Happen: How to Prepare Yourself and Others for Peak Performance." He sent it to me to review and it absolutely blew me away. You'll be reading from it soon, learning from a true master.

Several of my current and former clients want me to share their amazing stories with you. They come from a variety of backgrounds, have a range of personal pursuits and limiting issues, and all have traversed over the same territory that you will be covering. They were all trying to successfully reach their highest level of functioning, but they didn't know how to do that. In the meantime, they were experiencing self-sabotage, unforced errors, and careless mistakes.

When I start to train new clients, I begin with one of my questionnaires. I have different ones for different activities, such as athletic execution, musical performance, competitive gaming, and taking tests like the SAT, LSAT, and the bar exam. Within a very short period of time, these scientific assessments can give both my new client and myself an idea of their strengths and main areas for improvement. After the results are validated, I can offer them a practical plan for turning their weaknesses into strengths. The various assessments measure critical things like anxiety level, frustration tolerance, confidence, distractibility, motivation, mental toughness, and the ability to focus under extreme pressure. However, you will not need to take any of these assessments before heading out on your adventure.

There will be others who join you on this journey. Coach Ron O'Brien will be along on the trip to offer his guidance, experience, and knowledge. Another wise man who will join you on your journey is Professor Joseph Campbell. Joseph Campbell was a professor of cultural anthropology at Sarah Lawrence College in New York, and he studied diverse cultures throughout history. These cultures were separated by continents and oceans, thousands of years, and numerous native languages, nevertheless, they all shared remarkably similar stories and common myths.

Myths are stories that help societies make sense of the unknowable. Common themes revolve around human yearnings, fears, and aspirations, all of which are a part of life for all people. Creation myths attempt to explain the origins of humankind and where we came from. Similar narratives can be found in almost every culture in the world.

Campbell discovered that the most prevalent myth in every society, philosophy, and religion involves an ordinary person and their transformative adventure to rise above their day-to-day conditions, confront their issues, and become a true hero. The quest is known as the "hero's journey", and it follows a sequence of stages. It usually begins in the would-be hero's mundane world, stuck in what they feel is a boring and unfulfilling life without direction.

The ensuing adventure has three main parts. The first is departure, when the main character leaves the comfort of home and ventures into unfamiliar and threatening territory. The second is initiation, with a series of challenging trials and fierce opponents that the would-be hero must confront. The final part is returning home as a victorious hero, having endured rites of passage along the way. Home is still the same place, but the hero has been transformed through the process and is no longer the same.

Campbell wrote *The Hero with a Thousand Faces* in 1949. In 1973, a young screenwriter named George Lucas started writing the screenplay for a new kind of sci-fi adventure. After two years, he had written many scripts, none of which worked for him. Then he remembered what he'd learned from Campbell's book, which he'd read in college. He soon finished and released the first episode in the *Star Wars* series, based on Campbell's writings about the hero's journey. Here are the stages as they appear in the first *Star Wars* movie.

The Hero's Journey

Stage 1. Ordinary World: Luke Skywalker lives an ordinary existence working on his uncle's moisture farm on his home planet of Tatooine.

Stage 2. Call to Action: A messenger droid brings Princess Leia's plea to find Ben Kenobi and join the mission to save the Rebel Alliance from destruction.

Stage 3. Refusal of the Call: Luke is invited to join a dangerous mission. Luke says that he can't leave his uncle and aunt on some kind of space adventure.

Stage 4. Overcoming Resistance: Luke discovers that the Empire has killed his uncle and aunt. Obi Wan tells Luke about his Jedi heritage and the Force. He asks Luke to leave home and become Jedi.

Stage 5. Crossing the Threshold: Luke agrees to join the Rebel Alliance against the Empire. He pledges to go to Alderaan with Obi Wan and learn the ways of the Jedis, like his father before him.

Stage 6. New Conditions: On Alderaan, Luke begins lightsaber training, using a remote, moving training device. With his helmet's blast shield down, Luke learns to trust his feelings.

Stage 7. Deep Change: Han Solo's Millennium Falcon starship, with Obi Wan, Luke, and Chewbacca aboard, are pulled by a tractor beam into the Death Star.

Stage 8. The Ordeal: Inside the Death Star, Obi Wan goes to deactivate the tractor beam. Luke rescues Princess Leia, while Obi Wan sacrifices himself to Darth Vader.

Stage 9. The Reward: Luke has saved the Princess and captured the plans for the Death Star. They now have a way to defeat the Galactic Empire once and for all.

Stage 10. The Return: Heading back, they are attacked by Empire ships, but fend them off. They must return to the rebel base immediately and prepare for battle.

Stage 11. The Final Push: The rebels, with Luke as one of the pilots, take on Death Star. Luke trusts his feelings and fires the ultimate shot that destroys the Death Star.

Stage 12. Mastery: Luke and Han return to the rebel base after their triumph. They receive medals for their brave actions in the face of extreme danger. They are true heroes.

Get Ready for Your Journey

You will need a journal or separate notebook to accompany this book. It is very important that you write things out by hand. Putting a pen or pencil to paper is a powerful exercise that has a greater impact on your brain than typing on a device. Writing things down requires your full attention and engages both sides of your brain. It makes you more accountable for your actions and reinforces desired behavior and productive activities. It gets the thoughts, feelings, and experiences on paper, where you can see them objectively and make better sense of them. In the process, the act of writing leads to goal achievement and helps develop discipline and confidence.

Over the next several weeks, I will teach you exercises to help develop your confidence, courage, and execution of complex movement skills. The goal is to achieve your best performance ever by the end of week 4 or after you've completed the 21 steps. I trust that you are ready to embark on an exciting journey of understanding your highest levels of performance—especially in something that you already do at least fairly well.

There are several ways to approach this information. If you have an important event in about a month, follow this program closely day-by-day for the next four weeks, hopefully starting this coming Monday. That involves reading the written material and doing all the recommended exercises, which can take from 10–30 minutes every day. You will have one day off each week.

If you have more time to prepare, and/or you are relatively busy for the next month or two, you can go at a different pace. You can complete the course in 21 separate steps. If you take two or three days to complete each step, it will take you two or three months to complete the entire course. If you don't need to rush the process and have other important things going on in your life, you can take your time and better assimilate the information.

If you choose to read through the text first without doing the exercises, you will gain a lot of valuable information. Knowledge is power. That power will hopefully take you to a higher level of understanding of what causes unforced errors. After you understand, you can go back to the beginning of the book and do the exercises which will eliminate those unnecessary mistakes and help you achieve peak functioning.

Do not underestimate the challenge facing you. Get prepared for an exciting adventure into new and different territory on the path to your best. It is not meant to be easy or simple, but you will learn a lot about yourself, and you may also have some fun along the way. I will share everything that I know to get you ready for a flawless performance.

Let me introduce you to some folks who have already ventured into the journey that lies ahead of you. Parker became a PGA tournament-winning golfer who later needed to make a transition from golf to business. Jacqueline, Katy, and Dylan are all classical musicians who were struggling to win important auditions after many failed attempts.

You will also meet Alexa, from Washington. A few years ago, this wife and mother of five was studying for the bar exam when I took her on as a client. With about a month to go before the big test, she began freaking out. Her anxiety was through the roof. She was having problems studying and sleeping, and she was becoming more and more pessimistic about her chances.

Mia is a 20-something British undergraduate musician who had failed her first recital exam, an exam that was necessary for her to graduate. She was feeling really down and negative, as was Athina, another client who was also struggling with her music and herself. They were both having difficulty focusing, amongst other issues.

As a potential hero, you may be performing or competing at a relatively competent level, except for occasional, unexplained mistakes. Factoring those in, this level of performance could be regarded as relatively ordinary. If you're interested in moving to a higher level, consider yourself to be at the end of stage 1 in your hero's journey. This book signifies the start of stage 2. *Train Your Own Hero* is offering your call to action.

This is an invitation to leave your usual way of performing and begin the adventure of a lifetime. Imagine what it would be like to achieve the best performance of your life a month or so from now. Are you willing to explore the inner recesses of your mind in order to reach your peak level of functioning? This is the starting point for achieving a much higher level, with fewer or no unforced errors. Or you can refuse the call (stage 3) and remain at stage 1. However, if you're able to overcome your resistance to change (stage 4) you will soon cross the threshold (stage 5) by learning how to center, the first component of peak functioning.

You should first establish a baseline of your present level of performance, factoring in your current deficiencies. Write down what you think is holding you back from realizing your full potential in your chosen endeavor. What is not working well for you at this point? Could it be a lack of energy, consistency, willpower, focus, confidence, courage, or imagination? What do you need to change to perform significantly better? What do you need to improve or overcome to reach your peak level of functioning? Write out your answers in your journal or notebook.

The action of writing requires you to capture coherent and helpful thoughts. It retains a permanent record of your changing mindset and progress; it is much better than relying on your memory. To paraphrase Zen masters, "even a dull pencil is better than a sharp memory." Get in the habit of writing important things down, completing the recommended exercises, and noting your improvements for the next several weeks. You can start the adventure whenever you are ready. Go for it!

Monday or Step 1

*N*ow you'll learn about two of the seven components of peak functioning, the entering strategy and the optimistic mindset. You will meet the first of my former clients and I will discuss the issues she had, like performance anxiety, when we initially started working together. She will also be explaining in her own words what her experience was like. Finally, you will be starting your daily centering practice and learning how to develop a more optimistic outlook.

When I first met Mia, she was a student at the Royal College of Music in London, working on a Bachelor of Music degree in trumpet performance. She had a panic attack during her recital exam. Needless to say, it didn't go well. Mia recalls,

> At the end of my third year, I was filled with anxiety about my upcoming performance. COVID had put me out of performing in front of people, doing my classes as usual, seeing people face to face... Everything was suddenly isolated, and I hadn't performed in front of anyone for about six months. I was expected to do this big performance. I was absolutely terrified.
>
> Normally, our recitals are open to the public. Anyone can attend, and the adjudicators sit in the back. However, due to

COVID, there were only the five adjudicators and me. I've always had difficulties with my nerves, but at this event, my anxiety was at an all-time high. It was crazy. I had a panic attack in the middle of my recital. It was a bottom-of-the-pit low. I've just had the biggest failure ever with this massive thing, like it just happened.

After the recital, Mia described herself as feeling "the lowest of low that I had ever reached". It was only a few months before her senior recital, and she needed to take auditions for graduate programs and scholarships. She was struggling, wondering how she would accomplish everything she needed to do in a few short months. Her final recital would be a significant part of her degree, including 85% of the final grade, so it was a very stressful event for most music students. It was especially so for Mia. That's when she contacted me.

As I usually do with my new clients, I first listened to Mia's story and background, and then I asked her to take one of my online assessments that I use with performing artists to help understand their strengths and weaknesses. Unsurprisingly, she had an extremely high level of performance anxiety, with no ability to bring it under control. She felt pessimistic and struggled with low confidence, negative thinking, and an inability to focus, especially under pressure. Mia would need to learn how to focus by centering and then practicing this new skill. She would also need to develop an optimistic attitude and build her confidence and courage.

These are frequent starting points for my clients, and it's here that you will begin your hero's journey, too. This is how Mia described centering: "It was like a light bulb moment for me. It was a big help because it basically stopped the loud, distracting thoughts in my head. After I learned to center, the thoughts just switched off entirely. I use it quite literally as a tool before any time I play, I still do. It focuses my mind on what I need to do and blocks out anything that could distract me or affect my performance."

The Centering Process

Learning to center marks stage 5 in your hero's journey. Like Luke Skywalker, you're about to cross the threshold and begin to acquire powerful new strategies, practices, and exercises for achieving a higher level of functioning, far beyond the ordinary realm. I have used centering to train SWAT officers to perform better in stress shooting, Olympic athletes to win gold medals, and Grand Prix drivers to win series championships. One musician who won back-to-back professional auditions, including a principal position, called centering his "secret weapon".

There are two types of centering that you will learn in this program, centering down and centering up. Centering down is about bringing your nervous energy "down," so that you can focus on what you need to do in the moment. Centering up, which you will learn later, is about raising your energy up to get you ready for a big event.

Centering comes from the Japanese martial art aikido and modern-day sports psychology. Centering is effective for helping people perform their best under pressure for a number of reasons. First, it teaches conscious control over breathing, which can be adversely affected by stressful circumstances. Second, it releases the muscle tension that usually accompanies challenging situations. And third, centering triggers important mental shifts from the left hemisphere to the right.

The left hemisphere of the cerebral cortex is where we think in words and numbers. It's the noisy critic that will not shut up, the scatterbrain that cannot focus. It never runs out of analyses, comments, complaints, opinions, or worries. Conversely, the right brain is where we see images, hear sounds, and feel correct movements. It is the nonverbal, quiet side of the brain. The right hemisphere is much better than the left for focusing attention on accomplishing the task at hand.

Left vs. Right Brain

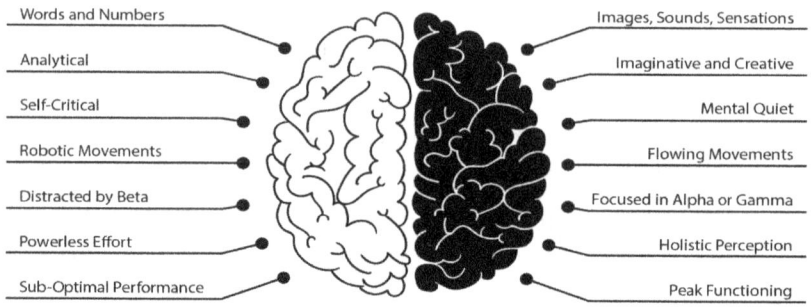

Words and Numbers	Images, Sounds, Sensations
Analytical	Imaginative and Creative
Self-Critical	Mental Quiet
Robotic Movements	Flowing Movements
Distracted by Beta	Focused in Alpha or Gamma
Powerless Effort	Holistic Perception
Sub-Optimal Performance	Peak Functioning

After you master centering down, you will be able to quickly shift from your left brain to your right. Working from your right brain, you will be able to clearly picture what you intend to do, hear it just the way you would like it to sound, and sense the way it feels when done correctly. It is critical that you always get into this right-brain state of mind before you perform or execute your skills, so that you can achieve peak functioning.

There are three phases in the centering down training, basic, intermediate, and advanced. Basic teaches you the seven steps of centering. It takes about a minute once you get used to it. The second phase is intermediate centering, and it builds on the first phase. Because you have already mastered the seven steps, you can jump into the process much more quickly. By the time you reach advanced centering, you'll have mastered both basic and intermediate, and you can center down in just a few seconds, anywhere, any time.

One of my clients, Dylan, a professional musician, described the different phases of centering this way: "If a quarterback is going to throw a pass, they are not thinking a bunch of steps for how to throw. They are just thinking about just a couple basic steps, right? All of the work to coordinate the body to throw well has already been done." With basic, Intermediate, and eventually advanced centering, it's the same thing.

"You've already done all the work to find your focal point, you know what your intentions are, and you're focused."

You can start learning the basic form of centering down right now or whenever you would like. When you do, start by finding a comfortable sitting position, with your back straight and feet solidly on the floor, so you feel grounded. Place your hands over your center, visualizing the space two inches below your navel and two inches in toward your spine. Make sure that you feel in balance, with your back straight. You can keep your head up or let your chin rest gently on your chest.

The first step in centering is to form a clear intention specifying what you would like to accomplish after you are centered. This could be, for example, to start out the competition well or to hit the high note at the end of the piece. For now, let your intention be to learn the seven steps of the centering process. Say to yourself, "now I am going to learn how to center."

The second step is to pick your focal point. This is a specific spot, three to seven feet in front of you, where you direct your full attention. It is important that you choose a focal point that is below your eye level. If you look up, it tends to put you into the left brain which is the last place you want to be as a performer. After focusing on your point, close your eyes.

The third step is to be mindful of your breathing. Pay close attention to your breathing, as you inhale slowly, in through your nose, pause, and then exhale slowly out through your mouth. Breathe slowly and deeply into your center. Feel your hands move in and out as they rest over your center and avoid letting your shoulders rise and fall. Take several breaths until you are focused only on your breathing.

The fourth step is to scan your body for muscle tension and then release it. Coordinate your scan with your breathing. On the inhale, check your jaw to see if it is tight. Feel free to move it around and then breathe out any tension you find. Then check your neck and throat, shoulders, arms, wrists, and hands. Finally, take one deep breath and release any tension that remains in your upper body.

The fifth step is to be at your center. The idea is to move from your left brain to the right by sensing your center, or at least sensing your hands from the inside. You want to be in touch with that quiet, still place. You can visualize it approximately two inches below your navel and two inches toward your spine. Or you could just picture that point as your core or center of gravity. However you do it, the idea is to get out of your head and into your center.

The sixth step is to vividly imagine the execution of your activity or performance going just the way you intend. Picture it exactly how you want it to go; hear it just the way you want it to sound and sense your body's movements being performed correctly.

The seventh step is to allow the energy to come up from your center, through your body, up and up, until it reaches your eyes. Then open your eyes and focus back on your point. You are now centered and ready to perform your best.

"Flow with whatever may happen and let your mind be free. Stay centered by accepting whatever you are doing." Chuang Tzu

Basic Centering Down

1. **Form your clear intention.** State what you intend to accomplish after you are centered.

2. **Pick your focal point.** Select an external point lower than eye level before closing your eyes.

3. **Start abdominal breathing.** Breathe slowly and deeply into your center.

4. **Scan for muscle tension.** Check for tightness, then breathe it out.

5. **Be at your center.** Get out of your head and into your center.

6. **Imagine it correctly.** See it, feel it, and hear it the way you intend.

7. **Direct your energy to your focal point.** Let the energy flow from your center to your focal point.

Practice this basic form of the centering process at least twice today and then even more times for the next several days. Keep track of each of the sessions, as well as your insights and progress in your journal or notebook. You will soon start to see significant changes in your mindset and your focus before you begin performing.

"Habit is stronger than reason." George Santayana

Token Economy

The best approach for motivating yourself to engage in productive behavior, like practicing the centering process, is with positive reinforcement. One powerful way to influence and reinforce voluntary actions is with a highly effective self-motivational system known as the token economy.

In a token economy, you reinforce every completed task or target behavior, like practicing centering, by using tokens. Tokens can be coins, marbles, gold stars in your journal or notebook or just checking off tasks you've accomplished on a white board. Whenever we accomplish a targeted task and receive positive reinforcement for doing so, like a token, it releases dopamine, a neurotransmitter in the brain. That makes us feel good and motivates us to engage in the desired behavior again and again.

After you accumulate a certain number of tokens, you can exchange them for tangible rewards. These rewards will serve as permanent and symbolic reminders of the effort and time that you spent to gain them. Katy, a musician, chose to purchase clothes that made her feel confident, such as a nice raincoat or a red sweater that made her feel good about herself and reminded her of the work she'd put in on her journey.

In general, the rewards should be tangible items that you really want, like decorations, clothes, jewelry, books, audio recordings, etc., rather than things you eat or drink that are soon forgotten. Of course, another client, Athina, did take herself out for a nice meal as a reward, because this kind of reward felt meaningful to her. The right reward can help you act in a proactive way that will help achieve your goals.

Receiving the reward needs to be contingent upon completing the specified number of targeted actions. You don't get the reward and symbol until you complete the requisite number of repetitions. Once you do complete them, make sure to reinforce the productive behavior as soon as possible with your justly deserved reward.

Be sure to thoughtfully consider what your tokens will be, what you need to do to earn them, how many tokens will be needed to exchange for a bigger reward, and exactly what that reward will be. A highly desired reward can change your willingness to do things that you would rather not do as you strengthen your willpower. For now, choose the reward that you will receive after you accumulate 21 tokens for practicing basic centering. The reward will reinforce your continuing progress, so you will be ready to move on to intermediate centering next week.

Being centered is the first component of peak functioning.

Skepticism

"We are very near to greatness: one step and we are safe; can we not take the leap?" Ralph Waldo Emerson

A skeptical mindset protects the ego from the fear of possible embarrassment or looking like a fool. However, it also prevents potentially helpful new ideas and information from being considered; skeptics lack the power of imagination. A cautious approach to new or different concept can delay or block important improvements. A suspicious attitude limits possible sources of knowledge, but new knowledge can be a real source of power. Skepticism limits understanding, preventing meaningful progress, personal growth, and peak functioning.

Skeptics have trouble believing in anything that they can't see, feel, or experience, in order not to be fooled. You be open-minded, rather than approaching unfamiliar things with skepticism, doubt, caution, and fear. Otherwise, it may take you a long time before you are able to reach peak functioning. I strongly suggest that you suspend your disbelief or skepticism for the next several weeks about what you think is possible for you. Be open to exploring new realms and your full potential.

Learning Optimism

"Pessimism leads to weakness, optimism to power." William James

An important aspect to achieve peak functioning is developing an optimistic mindset, or an attitude of positive expectancy. When optimists think about specific events in the future, they expect that things will go well. Despite potentially challenging conditions, adversity, or personal setbacks, they believe that good things will happen and that everything will work out for the best.

Here's how Mia described her shift to a more optimistic outlook: "One of the huge things we worked on from the get-go was my outlook on how I viewed my playing back then. It was a negative mindset. I had basically thought that if I'm not a good player, then I'm not a good human." Mia had merged her whole sense of self with her attitude towards herself as a musician, a common issue in the music world.

"The classical music world is so intense, and it is so competitive. If you're not successful in it, you're basically, well, it's insinuated that you're not good enough at anything. That's how it's put upon you. I had this idea that if I don't do it perfectly, I will crash and fall straight away. So, the first thing we started to work on was my left-brain self-talk and developing my optimism."

Optimists view problems as temporary challenges to overcome. They bounce back quickly from losses and setbacks; they see defeats as events to learn from and understand that many factors cause them. Optimists approach tough situations head-on, from a position of confidence and power. They view adversity as just another obstacle to move past on the way to achieving success. Once they do, optimists gain even more confidence in their ability to produce desired results.

On the other hand, pessimists interpret negative events as disappointing, discouraging, and long-lasting. They tend to blame themselves and others for their misfortunes, even those beyond their ability to control. They evaluate results as being either good or really bad, but most of the time they think their results are not good at all. Pessimists engage in a lot of negative, left-brain dialogue and self-criticism. Even when they are in their right brains, pessimists can do significant damage to their expectations of themselves by imagining all the things that could possibly go wrong. As you will see, though, what you think is what you get. If pessimism is getting you down, it's important to shift how you are thinking.

You can start today to override your dysfunctional pessimistic thought patterns. Over the next few weeks, you will learn to become much more optimistic and much less pessimistic, and you will receive all the benefits that will come with the shift.

To start, you must first understand your own habitual reactions to apparent difficulties and problems. In your journal or notebook, take some time to write down your usual thoughts when you are confronted with unfortunate circumstances, adversity, unwanted situations, mistakes, and failures. Do you find yourself criticizing yourself, others, or blaming circumstances before, during, or after unsuccessful ventures? Consider how those thoughts can cause unhelpful patterns and unwanted results.

After noting them, take some time to consciously challenge every pessimistic idea that you have about your ability to triumph over challenging circumstances, losses, adversity, and disappointment. Dispute each idea with real evidence and facts when you thought that things were really going against you. Make a strong argument on your own behalf. Write down your main points in your journal or notebook. Optimism does not guarantee success, but pessimism will always lead to failure. Optimism is the best way for you to reach peak functioning.

Here are some other ways for you to become more optimistic. Hopefully you realize how important this learned ability is for your continuing progress. However, while optimism doesn't guarantee success, pessimism will certainly cause you to perform far below your capabilities.

An optimistic mindset is the best way to realize your full potential. Here are ways to develop your optimism:

- Learn to look on the bright side of every event
- Recognize all your previous triumphs and successes under pressure
- Look for the opportunity in every challenge, difficulty, or problem that you are given
- Try to surround yourself with confident and optimistic people
- Accept whatever temporary circumstances you are in unconditionally
- Focus on what you can do to improve the most important and urgent things
- Believe totally in your talent, training, and experience
- Trust yourself unconditionally
- Always expect your best

In your journal or notebook, write out your own thoughts about optimism and a positive attitude. Map out a personal plan for becoming more positive about yourself and your unlimited potential. Right now, the main things standing in the way of your highest levels of functioning are your own limiting beliefs, including those fueled by fear and skepticism. To do your best, you will need to maintain a positive, optimistic mindset, always expecting your best.

A positive mindset is the second component of peak functioning.

Here are some of Coach Ron O'Brien's thoughts about this component:

> Keep a positive attitude! You hear this all the time, but it is true that rarely does anything good happen when your attitude goes south. Train yourself to utilize positive self-talk. The important thing to remember about a positive attitude is it counts the most when things are not happening the way you would like.

Frustration generally occurs when a series of things don't go the way you would like them to. One situation that frequently results in frustration occurs when you are trying to perform a task or learn a skill. You make several attempts, and nothing is working. The same scenario of negative self-talk and that sinking feeling starts. How you react to this situation determines whether you can move past the frustration and return to a positive approach, or whether you continue down the negative road and maybe carry it through the whole day. If you don't turn your attitude around, you become unproductive. That makes reaching your potential harder.

Adversity is different from frustration. Frustration is situational, whereas adversity is created by an obstacle in your path to succeeding at something, a roadblock you must find a way around in order to achieve the results you are seeking.

Once you have identified your roadblock to success, the mental way you respond to it is the key to overcoming it. There are two ways you can react. One is negative and the other is positive. One saps your energy and motivation, the other increases them. The negative response is to view what is in front of you as an obstacle, one that allows you to make excuses for not succeeding. The positive response is to view the obstacle as a challenge. This should spur you to think and work harder. You need to learn to accept adversity as a challenge to prove that you can persevere and find a way through it. The challenge is to prove to yourself that you are tough enough to overcome it and do your best.

Here are my recommendations for what you should doing today or during this first step as you begin your trek:

- Think about your current level of performance
- Consider what may be keeping you from your best

- Practice basic centering at least 2 times
- Examine what you're skeptical about
- Suspend your disbelief about your full potential
- Write down your negative thoughts
- Challenge them with evidence and facts
- Write out your positive thoughts
- Start to develop your optimism
- Always expect your best

Week 1

Tuesday or Step 2

*W*elcome to your second day or step of your hero's training. Now you will learn about change, the elements of self-confidence, and the left and right hemispheres of the brain. Specifically, we'll be talking about the self-talk and inner dialogue that goes on in your left brain when you are executing your skills. We'll also learn about fear-based thinking, outcome thinking, and process thinking.

Fear of Change

"Progress is impossible without change, and those who cannot change their minds cannot change anything." George Bernard Shaw

One of the main reasons for resistance is the fear of change. Fear causes people to want to remain in their comfort zone, in the safety of familiar circumstances, even if those aren't working well for them. Some people fear that the changes that they are trying to make will never work. Others may worry that even if they work, it won't make much of a difference in the end. These fears are understandable, but they are very counterproductive.

If you are interested in making major improvements in your skills, you will need to get past your own natural resistance to change. Even if it's for the better, most people cringe or recoil at the thought of altering their usual way of doing things. Also, change rarely produces immediate improvements. In fact, change often causes refined skills to get worse before they get better. Change is usually disruptive and uncomfortable, and dramatic improvement cannot always be guaranteed. That's why change is universally met with such resistance.

However, change is part of the natural order of things. Nothing alive can remain stagnant for any amount of time and still exist. If we define change as the altering of positions, conditions, or configurations, everything in life is constantly moving. Everything that continues to live adapts, moves, and evolves. If you reflect on the major changes in your life, you will see that most or all of them were for the better, although you may not have realized it at the time.

It is time to embrace the inevitable process of transformation so you will be able to peak your skills when you need to. You must change several things by then if you want to reach your best past your resistance. In the meantime, change your thoughts about the important process of change. Rather than trying to resist, avoid, or prevent change, the idea is to create change for the better for yourself. You can start with changing your level of confidence and trust in your abilities. Coach O'Brien writes,

> There are two cornerstones of progress and achievement. You must be changing constantly and learn to accept change. This doesn't mean you need to change everything day after day. It means after you have given a certain way of doing something an adequate trial and the results aren't productive, you need to look for some other method or technique.

> This is when you have a pool of information from which to draw when making that change. Trial and error many times provide the new information necessary for you to have a real breakthrough. Being willing to experiment and take chances with new approaches is necessary to continue to move forward. Sometimes you must use several trials and make several errors before you hit on the approach that works. This requires

analysis, imagination, and innovation. Just keep at it until you find the answer.

With regard to natural ability, it is not necessary that it is developed at the highest level, but that you have enough ability so that hard work, persistence and determination can make up for what you are lacking. As a coach, I have seen time after time that a person with good ability, but a strong passion and work ethic can achieve a higher level of success than the person with great natural talent who lacks those other qualities.

My client Alexa needed to dramatically change her level of confidence and trust in her abilities before an important upcoming event. When we first met, she was a law clerk studying for the bar exam. She had a master's degree in social work, but she wanted to become a practicing attorney to help people with estate planning. She had never attended law school and instead had qualified to sit for the bar exam by completing a mentoring program with an attorney. She had finished that program a few months prior, and the exam was then less than two months away.

She hired another attorney who specialized in helping candidates prepare for the bar. However, with six weeks to go, Alexa was very pessimistic about her chances of passing. She was having problems studying and focusing on practice tests, constantly second-guessing herself, and worrying about failing. Her confidence was very low, and she had many serious doubts. Her anxiety was through the roof, but she had no effective strategies for bringing it under control.

When she explained her story to me, it was easy to understand why she was freaking out. Alexa explained, "It's a very formidable exam that a lot of very smart people don't pass. I have my own set of insecurities that I'm working through. I'm a perfectionist, and I wanted to pass the exam on the first try." Thinking back on those months, she remembered that she had been "putting a lot of pressure on myself and feeling so out of control, I guess that I knew it just wasn't working. Like I was heading for a crash, emotionally speaking. I wasn't handling it very well."

Her exam was scheduled for the third week of July. It would take place in a large room with lots of other hopefuls. She had started studying intensely for the test in May, which had been a rough month for her. She reached out to me in early June. I drew up a schedule and concrete approach to the studying that she still needed to do. This helped Alexa handle the increasing anxiety and all thoughts that were racing around in her head.

Specifically, she learned how to counteract the negative thoughts that she was having and shift from a negative to a positive mindset. In her words, she said:

> I just really liked having the structural framework for that, instead of just feeling like I was flailing around in those repetitive thoughts. We did a lot of mindset work addressing my fears. My mindset was very negative and fearful. I was feeling like I'm not sure I can even do this, maybe I don't even deserve to have a chance of success. Don taught me that first I had to accept that I felt that way and just say yes to my situation.

> Instead of bringing negativity to everything, I was developing my optimism with a much more positive mindset. There was a lot of monitoring and writing out my negative thoughts and changing them more and more into positives. I could feel my confidence grow and that was really helpful to me at the time.

I taught Alexa basic centering and told her to practice it several times a day, especially before she started studying or taking practice tests. I also asked her to monitor her internal dialogue and self-talk. She wrote down all the things she said to herself that she wouldn't say to a good friend or a student who she was tutoring. Writing it down helped her change the words she said to herself and think instead about positive statements she'd say to a good friend. Then she would repeat the new statements out loud several times.

This activity is just one of the things that helped raise Alexa's level of confidence and her trust in her new abilities in the legal profession. You're about to learn more about how to raise your own level of confidence. But first, you need to understand how the left and right sides of our brains work and how this connects to your internal monologue or self-talk. All of this will help you improve your confidence and execute any activity that requires a high level of performance, whether that's taking an exam, performing in a recital or audition, or shooting a low score in golf.

Self-confidence

Your level of confidence and ability to unconditionally trust yourself under pressure is the direct result of three main factors: positive self-talk, imagining your best, and striving for excellence.

Self-talk

"There is nothing either good or bad but thinking makes it so." William Shakespeare

Your self-talk is how you talk to yourself in words. It may include criticism, unnecessary instructions, running commentary, analyzing mistakes, thinking about missing a note or goal, and telling yourself what to do or not to do. The more you think about missing a note (or telling yourself not to miss it), the more likely it is that you will miss it. After that happens, you may get very critical about your mistake and think even more unhelpful things inside your mind.

My music students at Juilliard often said awful things to themselves while performing. "Why do you suck so bad?" an outstanding pianist used to say to herself. "Don't miss the freakin' entrance!" a talented violinist would remind herself. "Great! Now everybody thinks you look like a fool," another student heard in her head after a missed note. Most of them relied on a motivational system that was more "stick" than "carrot."

Even if you have achieved success through the "stick" approach, from this point forward in your career, you can create less wear and tear on your nervous system by using a more "carrot-like" positive approach. At this point, you need to understand how your negative internal dialogue affects you as well as your performance.

The things you repeat to yourself during stressful circumstances register cumulatively in your mind. Since you are saying it to yourself, you probably don't filter any of it out. Instead, you absorb what you think. Even if you are not beating yourself up, if you tell yourself over and over not to mess up, you hear yourself talk about messing up.

All these words are more important than you may think. Consider the difference between the words "difficult" and "challenging." These two words can produce very different outcomes. If you view a task or situation as "difficult," you will likely find it to be exactly that way. Your own thoughts put you into a victim mentality, making you think about the difficulty of the task rather than for your ability to remedy it or solve the problem.

If you view a situation as a challenge, though, you can consider it as an opportunity to develop your abilities in that area or prove your talent. The exact same situation, depending upon the language you use to describe it, can change immediately into an event that you can use to help you improve or just show off. The shift in thinking is important because people tend to talk constantly about important upcoming projects and events. Words are thoughts expressed.

Whether spoken aloud or just said in your mind, these words have a dramatic effect on your subconscious mind and your self-confidence. Although it is extremely powerful, your subconscious will believe anything you tell it, especially things that you say over and over. Your subconscious does not care if you say something to yourself or to others. Each time you repeat something, it emphasizes on producing that result. Furthermore, the subconscious is very literal. Even if you say something as a joke, your subconscious accepts it literally as a matter of fact.

There is one more important fact about your subconscious. This very powerful part of your mind, where your self-confidence resides, does not process the words "don't" or "do not," only what comes after the command. Consider the implications of such often-repeated statements as "don't get off to a bad start," or "don't mess that part up." Your subconscious only hears, "get off to a bad start," or "mess that part up." That is not the message you want to be sending. These thoughts happen a lot during stressful circumstances, and they tend to cause problems. The good news is that you can change negative thought patterns into more helpful ones.

The first step in developing positive self-talk is to examine the specific language that you use when you are performing. Monitoring and changing the content of your thoughts takes motivation, willingness, and an effective plan of action for how to do it. The solution starts with a written exercise. Today and during this step, write out all of your negative self-talk word for word, and then convert it to more positive language.

As you go about your daily activities, simply notice the negative things you say over and over to yourself. Write these comments down in your journal or notebook, but, as I explain in the next paragraph, leave space next to them to convert them to more positive thoughts and instructions. Rather than saying, "don't miss it," use a positive cue such as "nail it," or "Focus." Instead of thinking about what you *don't* want to happen, say the positive cue to yourself and focus on the process. You can handle those critics, blamers, and naysayers!

Each page should have two columns. In the left-hand column, write out anything unhelpful that you said to yourself. In the right-hand column, across from those comments, rewrite the unhelpful statements as positive instructions or thoughts.

Keep this up for the next several days, and you will find that you have replaced your worst cynics with a supportive team of encouraging allies and friends cheering you on. You deserve this! That shift in language will help raise your level of self-confidence. It did for both Mia and

Alexa as they started to switch their internal self-talk from negative to positive.

The next step in the process is to learn to use affirmations.

Affirmations

"All we are is the result of what we have thought. The mind is everything. What we think, we become." Buddha

One of the best ways to shift your mind in the direction of peak functioning is by repeatedly verbalizing the right kind of positive thoughts to yourself. These powerful words, known as affirmations, can have a dramatic effect on your confidence level and focus. Affirmations deliver clear directions and succinct messages directly to your subconscious. This amazing programming tool can help you overcome doubts, silence your inner critics, change your outlook, and keep your mind focused on what's important.

If you have never used affirmations before, saying them to yourself may seem a little corny at first, especially if your inner dialogue has been predominantly pessimistic, self-critical, or preoccupied with failure. Affirmations are optimistic and self-supporting declarations focused on progress or success. The language may be similar to assurances that you would give to a good friend before their big event. Or it could be like encouraging endorsements that you would want to hear from a respected colleague or teacher before you go on.

There are four types of affirmations. The first is a statement of perceived fact, such as "it's getting better all the time," or "it's going to go well." The second is a stated claim of ownership, like "my skills are getting better and better day-by-day!" The third type of affirmation is a you statement, as if it were someone else: "you can do it," or "you've got this!" Saying these positive things to yourself, rather than scattered and negative left-brain noise, will improve your confidence and focus.

The fourth and final type is the most powerful thing you can say to your subconscious, and it begins with the words "I am." Whatever you say after "I am" defines you and your limitations, as well as what you can achieve. These pronouncements need to resonate as true for you right now and in the near future. They should not be unrealistic ("I am the best in the world") or final ("I will never be better than this.") They should be said with deliberate intention, strong conviction, and enthusiasm.

Affirmations work best when they are written out and then said aloud on a daily basis. They become even more powerful when you say them in front of a mirror. You need to continue reciting your affirmations until you totally believe what you are saying is true now or about to happen in the very near future.

You want to find affirmations that truly resonate with you, that you can say with strong conviction. Try lots of them out until you find the right ones. The right affirmations can have a very powerful influence on your level of self-confidence and performance. Here are some suggestions for you to start:

- I'm becoming a more optimistic person
- You can do whatever you put your mind to
- I'm able to embrace change in my life
- I am becoming more and more confident
- My self-talk is getting more positive
- I can feel my confidence growing day by day
- I'm learning how to center myself in the here and now
- I'm trusting my talent and abilities more and more
- I'm working towards peak functioning every day
- I can imagine myself achieving my very best
- I know it's on the way

Better yet, come up with your own list of affirmations. Write them out in your journal or notebook. Say them out loud in the morning, hopefully in front of a mirror, and also throughout your day. You will soon notice their powerful effect on your positive outlook and self-confidence.

Fear-based Thinking

"Nothing is so much to be feared as fear." Henry David Thoreau

Fear-based thinking means imagining the worst. It's similar to walking on a wooden plank that is five inches thick, three feet wide, and twenty feet long. At the moment, the plank is lying on the ground. If I were to ask you to walk from one end of the board to the other, you would think it was no big deal. It is no big deal, but I would ask you to humor me and just try it. You do, and you tell me that you could walk the plank forward or backward, without a second thought.

This plank, however, is like being at home in a very safe environment, with no real consequences for mistakes or failure. However, high-pressure events have real consequences. It's as if we took the same wooden plank and put it between two skyscrapers, 300 feet up in the air. Things would change. Your usual, natural way of walking the plank would likely change. You would probably become more tentative, careful, and restricted, with lots of muscle tension. You may also start to look down, thinking about where you might land if you tripped and fell.

There are three main ways to think about walking the plank. The first is fear-based thinking or imagining the worst. As you probably realize by now, fear-based thinking is never recommended. It raises your anxiety levels and increases muscle tension, making falling much more likely to happen. Not a good idea, whether you're performing a recital, taking the bar exam, or standing three-hundred feet in the air, about to walk between two skyscrapers.

Outcome Thinking

"I never think of the future. It comes soon enough." Albert Einstein

The second type of thinking you might use when executing a skill is called outcome thinking: the need for you to get to the end of the plank or achieve a certain goal, like finishing a performance or winning a contest or game.

This thought process is a better way to think when you're walking the plank or in the middle of a performance or contest, but it still puts pressure on you to accomplish something in the future. It still emphasizes something that's out of your control, like getting to the end of the plank or performance or test. That end, however, is not yet a guaranteed result. In the meantime, you still must get through the event or walk the plank.

Both fear-based thinking *and* outcome thinking will affect your way of walking and make falling more likely. There's a much better way to successfully walk the plank or execute your performance skills under pressure, and that approach is called process thinking.

Process Thinking

"When walking, walk. When eating, eat." Zen maxim

Process thinking focuses in the here and now, on what you need to do. These are under your total control. Process thinking is concerned with executing the fundamentals in the continuing moment, rather than thinking about negative or future results. When you are under pressure, focus on the process and keep your mind in the present. Do not think about the future outcome that is presently out of your immediate control. Focus your mind on walking on the board the way you usually walk, with your eyes up and without overthinking.

Process thoughts are often phrased in simple language, like "Smooth," "Focus," or "Stay with it." These process cues are directly related to your best functioning in the continuing present moment in the here and now. Those kinds of verbal cues will help you remain focused exclusively on the task at hand. If you're going to think any words at all, words like these are the best ones to cue your highest level of execution under pressure.

Here are the things that I would recommend that you do on the second day of your journey:

- Practice basic centering at least 3 times
- Continue developing your optimism

- Improve your self-talk
- Write out your affirmations
- Say your affirmations out loud in front of a mirror three times
- Write out your fear-based thoughts related to your upcoming event
- Write out your outcome thoughts
- Write out your process cues
- Always expect your best

Wednesday or Step 3

*N*ow you will meet two amazing athletes and learn how they used their powerful and imaginative right brains to maximum advantage in major sports competitions. You will also discover how to increase your level of self-confidence through mental rehearsal and by building your volition or willpower.

My long-time client and good friend Parker had played volleyball and basketball as a high-school student growing up in Honolulu. But golf was his real passion. He was a very right-brained golfer who played with an exquisite sense of feel. He was recruited by several division 1 college teams and attended UCLA on a scholarship. He was a "decent golfer" in his four years, including some second-place finishes, but never a first-place finish while in college. After graduation, he had surgery on his injured left wrist that was the crux point of his golf swing.

I met Parker just after his surgery when I moved to Hawaii after 9/11. He still had a cast on his wrist and wouldn't be able to swing a golf club or even putt for months. Although he couldn't work as a golfer during that time or do much of anything else, he could learn as much as he could about sports psychology, the mental game of golf, and how to win. That's where I came in. While his physical game was on hold, we could work on improving his mental game.

For two months, we met several times a week and focused on helping Parker imagine everything he could about his golf game. Even though he couldn't physically play golf, he could imagine it. He pictured himself hitting great shots and feeling himself make long putts. Doing this helped Parker switch from thinking about his golf swing or putt in his left brain to seeing it and feeling it in his right brain.

We also worked on his pre-shot routines. After his cast was removed, we started with his putting routine. We covered all the things that he needed to do before hitting a putt, like reading the line and committing to his read. Next, he would take several rehearsal swings to get a feel for the right distance to the hole. Then he imagined the putt going down the intended line and dropping into the hole. He went through the routine several times in his mind before we ever tried it out on the practice green.

I placed three balls about twenty feet from the hole. Parker hadn't hit a putt for months. The average for PGA tour players from that distance is 14%. He made the first two putts and lipped out on the third one. Wow! Over the next two months, Parker started applying what he had learned to his short game shots around the green, like chips and pitches, and then to his full swing before playing entire rounds of golf. Before long, he began to compete in tournaments again, starting with local events in Hawaii. He started playing the best golf of his life. Four months later, he turned pro. Between 2003 and 2006, Parker won four times in other pro-tour events and even qualified to play in the US Open Championship. In 2007, Parker earned full playing status on the PGA Tour.

Mental Rehearsal

"You have to expect things of yourself before you can do them." Michael Jordan

Mental rehearsal is another principal way to increase your level of self-confidence. As you probably realized after reading about Parker's experiences, mental rehearsal means imagining the ideal execution of your skills through visualization. This is a powerful right-brain skill that is easy to learn and requires no physical effort whatsoever. It will help you achieve the best execution of your skills by first rehearsing them in your mind. When practiced correctly, this process can dramatically increase your level of trust in your own abilities, which will lead, in turn, to creating the performance outcomes that you desire and intend.

Before and during a big event, your imagination can run wild and get completely out of control. It can fill your head with disaster scenarios in which you have a serious error or fail. If these images are allowed to freely play out in your imagination, they can cause real damage, not just to your confidence, but to the actual performance and perhaps even lead to injury. That is why it is so important to continually imagine the *ideal* execution of your skills in your mind to override the doomsday videos.

To learn mental rehearsal, arrange for ten minutes alone in a quiet setting. Pick a time when you are alert. If you try this exercise when you are sleepy, you will probably drift off to sleep, and it will be about as useful as putting a textbook under your pillow at night! Just in case you do drift off, set an alarm for 12 minutes and turn off all other devices, notifications, or alerts.

You can practice this powerful technique either sitting in a chair or lying down. Just make sure that your back is relatively straight and that you feel comfortable. Remember to center, taking extra care to make sure that all your muscles are totally relaxed from head to toe before you begin.

How to Practice Mental Rehearsal

1. With your eyes closed, select a visual reference point. Vividly imagine one specific place in the room or a single object. It could be the doorknob in the room or one of your tokens. Try to see it as clearly as possible in your mind's eye. At first, the image may not have much detail, or you may have trouble bringing it into focus. This is normal. Your mental acuity will improve with a small amount of practice.

2. Begin slowly imagining your usual warm-up. If you're a musician, it could be playing scales or arpeggios. For golfers, it could be taking practice swings hitting a tee in the ground. Singers and presenters could warm up their voices. For dancers, it could be

stretching or rehearsing certain steps. Whatever it is, imagine doing it until you can hear it clearly, see it vividly, and feel it fully. Just like when you are getting ready. If this type of mental practice or visualization is new to you, take your time.

3. Make sure that you see yourself warming up from inside-out (like you're looking out at the music or golf tee) and outside-in (like you're watching yourself play or swing). When you can vividly imagine yourself going through your warmup in complete detail, seeing it clearly from inside-out and outside-in, as well as hearing the sounds and feeling the movements, you are ready to move on to the next step.

4. If you're a musician, select a relatively easy piece of music that you will imagine playing. Golfers can choose a tee shot on a short par. Presenters and singers can think of the opening lines of their best speeches or favorite songs. Dancers can imagine specific routines.

5. Whatever the activity, make sure that you can imagine yourself starting to execute the relevant skills correctly. You need to be able to clearly see yourself making the initial proper movements from inside and out, hear the opening lines or notes just the way you want them to sound, and fully feel yourself executing your skills flawlessly.

6. After you can see, hear, and feel yourself getting off to a great start, continue to imagine yourself executing your skills to the best of your ability. Gradually increase the difficulty of the activity, with more challenging repertoire, speeches, or golf shots, until you start imagining making mistakes. This is normal, especially if you're new to this type of practice.

7. If and when you do see, feel, or hear yourself make a mistake, hit the "stop" button in your mind. Rewind to a place in the action a short time before the error. Start from there, and move slowly at a speed you can control, so that it is correct. Increase the speed

gradually, as long as it is under your control, until you can vividly see, hear, and feel the skill executed correctly in real time.

8. In subsequent mental rehearsal practice sessions, work through your entire repertoire, presentation, speech, or different golf shots in 12-minute segments. The more often that you can vividly imagine the ideal execution of your skills, the more your confidence will increase. Before too long, your actual performance will accurately reflect your higher level of confidence in your abilities.

Practice mental rehearsal at least once a day for 5–10 minutes for the next several days. Keep track of your mental practice sessions in your journal or notebook. As with any learned skill, the quality will get better with repeated, correct practice over time. Set up a token economy for your mental rehearsal practice, including different tokens and rewards for completing 21 repetitions. By then, you will realize the tremendous benefits, including a significant increase in your confidence level and ability to perform to the best of your ability.

To help you understand the power of mental rehearsal, I'm going to introduce Olympic diver Greg Louganis to you. He is a master of this technique also known as visualization. Like Parker, he is extremely right brained. I met Greg in 1984 at the Mission Viejo pool in Southern California, when I started working with four-time Olympic diving Coach Ron O'Brien and his divers. They were preparing for the upcoming US Olympic trials, which were less than two months away.

Greg was born and raised in San Diego. He was adopted out of foster care when he was only nine months old. He started taking dance, acrobatics, and gymnastics lessons before he was two years old and, by the time he was three, he was giving public dance and acrobatic performances. That is when he started visualizing his performances. One day, his dance teacher got frustrated with him. She turned on the music in the studio and told the very young Greg to figure it out, leaving him alone in the room to imagine it going well.

He recollects, "It took several tries, but I got it. Then she said, 'make it fluid' and she left again. It took four times for me to get it fluid, because there were some transitions I didn't quite get, or I was late. She came back in the room and increased the tempo of the music as I visualized it, faster than I was going to perform the moves. It only took one shot, one try, before I was able to visualize it being fluid even at a faster tempo. I didn't know the importance of that until much later in my life."

Greg also didn't quite realize what he'd tapped into. As he says, "a three-year-old's imagination is just crazy, you know. There's no limit to a three-year-old's imagination, you can fly on a magic carpet. You can! There's all of those things that we did in our heads as children in that wonderful playground in your mind." When Greg visualizes today, he taps into what he started doing when he was only three years old, which is triggering the imagination in the right brain.

He says, "visualization is great, especially when you are first learning a new skill. You can go through the movements and feel them in slow motion. What muscles are triggering? How is my body moving? What am I seeing in my mind? What exactly is working? How do I coordinate everything together to connect? You need to make all those connections within your body and then imagine that skill in real time or even faster."

Willpower

"Great things are not something accidental but must certainly be willed." Vincent van Gogh

To raise your level of performance from this point on, you need to take meaningful action. Meaningful action means making real changes that only you can make. You are the primary agent of change in your life. Your ability to create significant change depends on the strength of your willpower or willful volition. Willful volition is your decision to act in certain ways in the present so that you will achieve established goals in the future. Where there's a will, there's a way.

Greg Louganis had high confidence and strong willpower because he earned it. He had impeccable practice habits. He came to the pool every day ready to do his best. He paid close attention to what his beloved coach wanted him to do. Greg tried to make every dive count, as if he was doing it in a major competition. He was one of the last divers to leave practice every day, and he spent considerable time away from the pool visualizing his dives, even choreographing them to music.

Just like Greg, the way to increase your willpower is to consciously make a series of correct choices about your daily behaviors. You may not become an Olympic diver, but your choices will help you on your hero's journey toward peak functioning. These behaviors include your diet and the amount of exercise, water, sleep, and rest that you get. Each positive or helpful decision progressively builds your personal power to control the execution of your skills and the ultimate results.

Volition involves the continual struggle between your rational and emotional sides about voluntary behavior. It is the never-ending battle between your thoughts about what you need to do versus what you feel like doing in the present moment. You strengthen your volition and will-power by choosing in the moment to do the correct thing that is in line with your long-term goals, even if you don't feel like it at the present time.

Volition is like a muscle. It grows stronger by making a series of correct decisions followed by physical actions, each of which builds your personal willpower. You will get in the habit of saying "yes" to actions that will help you improve and "no" to things that will delay or prevent your progress. Rather than taking the path of least resistance, doing the correct thing requires real effort, exerted repeatedly over time.

Like weight training, each time you use your "will" power instead of your "won't" power, it increases your inner strength. Choose to do the right thing despite what you might prefer. Say, "I will," instead of "I won't," or "I don't wanna." Consciously decide to override negative thinking and resistance by reminding yourself about what you want to accomplish in the end, namely achieving peak functioning.

Each time you decide to take meaningful action past apathy, fear, and resistance, your willpower and self-confidence will get stronger. You will come to believe more and more in yourself and trust your abilities.

Over time, with frequent correct decisions and increased challenges, you will feel even more confident and powerful. That will translate into more control of your execution and the results you are ultimately able to attain.

High self-confidence is the third component of peak functioning.

These are the things that I would recommend that you do on the third day or step of your journey towards peak functioning:

- Practice basic centering at least four times
- Continue developing your optimism
- Make your self-talk positive
- Say your most effective process cues out loud several times
- Say your cues to yourself as you are practicing performing
- Practice mental rehearsal at least three times
- Keep notes about your mental practice sessions
- Write down three things you are doing to build your willpower
- Imagine your ideal execution
- Always expect your best

Week 1

Thursday or Step 4

$\mathcal{N}$ow you will learn about strengthening your courage, the next component of peak functioning. Bravery is not the absence of fear; it's doing the very thing you fear so you can move beyond it. The key is to get ready to confront your fears, first in a safe environment, and then to subject them to increasing pressure. We will begin with small steps just outside your comfort zone, then progressively take on more risks past your fears, as you strengthen your courage.

Courage is the fourth component of peak functioning.

"Without courage, we cannot practice any other virtue with consistency." Maya Angelou

After many years training Olympic divers, SWAT officers, race car drivers, and auditioning musicians, I have learned that courage is always the best choice, especially under pressure. Fear never works in situations where there are serious consequences for mistakes or failure. It takes a soldier's valor to triumph over one's fears. Fortunately, you can develop your courage without joining the military. You just need to learn and practice ways to get past your limiting fears.

One client who has had success moving past her fears is Jacqueline, a professional bassoonist from the Midwest. When we first spoke in 2003, she was freelancing all over the region and taking orchestral auditions.

She had reached the semi-final rounds of some auditions, and even the finals for a few, but she still had not gotten a job.

Through my performance assessments, we determined that Jacqueline was extremely motivated, driven, committed, and able to focus her mind intensely. Her weaknesses, however, were holding her back, and those included low confidence, perfectionism, and being very self-critical. She had a lot of energy spiking at key moments that was hard to bring down to a more manageable, helpful level. She carried a lot of fear and unhelpful left-brain self-talk. We knew she needed to develop her courage, respond better to high-stress situations, and perform up to her full potential.

Jacqueline had a big audition coming up, the most important one that she had ever taken. She had decided that this was going to be a "make it or break it," that if this one didn't work out, she would follow another path outside of music. She recalls, "I had really never done any of the techniques or had even heard of any of the methods. I wasn't sure that it was going to work for me." For Jacqueline, it took courage to even try the methods that I teach.

She felt extremely skeptical that practicing without her instrument was going to work. She recalls, "He had to really coerce me to try it, I remember. I did, and it didn't go well the first time or two. I wasn't used to it. I was having a hard time getting right-brain enough so that I could focus on the music and not be distracted with left-brain thoughts like, 'I don't know if this is going to work,' or all the self-talk and the other stuff that goes on in my head."

It took Jacqueline a few times to get the hang of mental rehearsal, but eventually she realized it was working. "The first couple of times I did it, it was very awkward, and it probably didn't work that well. But Dr. Greene kept telling me, just do it, just do it. It'll get easier. And it did. I used a lot of mental rehearsal preparing for my audition. I imagined playing the music. I would do it 10 or 20 minutes a day. I would work on the key parts of the audition excerpts and just hear them going beautifully. After a while, it started to become much more natural."

While we were working on mental rehearsal, we also worked on Jacqueline's ability to believe in herself, changing her self-talk to be less negative and more positive, becoming more optimistic and getting from practice mode to performance/audition mode. Jacqueline recalled that after a while everything we worked on started to come together, "each one by itself was sort of like a piece of a puzzle or a bead on a full necklace that was ultimately coming together."

The next piece in the puzzle for Jacqueline and me to solve was her performance anxiety and fear. First, she needed to understand how fear affected her and her performance in high-pressure situations like auditions. Then she would need to start exercises to strengthen her courage. I knew that she already had courage, even if she had forgotten the fact, or she never would have persevered past her fear to make it this far. She just needed to learn how to further build upon that courage.

Understanding Fear

"Nothing in life is to be feared. It is only to be understood." Marie Curie

Fear is our natural response to perceived threats, danger, or loss. Performers and athletes fear the loss of opportunity, like failing an audition or not winning a gold medal. We fear the possibility of never achieving our dreams or falling short of our true potential. It is surprisingly common, also, to fear winning or achieving success.

Most people are raised to live in fear. We are taught from an early age that the world is not a safe place: Be careful, especially around strangers. Don't run with that stick, you'll poke your eye out! Don't climb the tree, you'll fall and break your arm. My father used to remind me to be cautious because, as he would say, "it's a dog-eat-dog world out there."

You were also probably taught to be cautious and avoid dangerous situations, which is wise when there is the possibility of real danger or physical harm. But in the process, you may have also learned to be overly cautious in all circumstances, even those that are not dangerous or life-threatening. In these situations, fear is not a helpful warning of potential danger; it is a major impediment to doing your best.

Fear's energy can make you feel like shrinking, like you want to run and hide. It inhibits movement and tends to shut things down. It prevents coordinated physical movements from flowing smoothly. Fear can take your confidence and personal sense of power away. It can make you feel like a helpless victim of forces beyond your control. It can cause you to perform defensively, setting you up to fail or to perform far below your true capabilities.

The feeling of fear will never go away if you continue to grow. You need to stretch your capabilities by taking healthy new risks beyond your comfort zone. The only way to get past your fear is to do what you fear. You are going to experience fear under pressure, but so is everyone else. The real issue is how you respond to it. Working through fear and taking healthy risks is not as bad as living with the feeling of powerlessness that accompanies fear. The first step is to understand the sources of your own performance fears and your usual responses to them.

Most people worry that something will happen that they won't be able to handle. But if you're still pursuing your career, you must have handled many things satisfactorily. Even if you're a student, you have handled your fears well enough to continue this far. It is easy to forget those occasions when you used your courage and to only recall the times when you did not handle your fear very well. For today's activity, I'd like you to write down your prior history of brave actions in your journal or notebook. I call this your courage history.

Courage History

"Courage is resistance to fear, mastery of fear – not absence of fear." Mark Twain

Start a new section in your journal or notebook. First, take time to recall all the circumstances, locations, situations, events, and people that caused you to feel fearful in the past. Then, write down seven events when you used your courage effectively and handled your fears.

Think specifically of those times and places where you took brave steps towards success rather than following the fear-based path to failure and loss of personal power. These events need not involve physical feats like bungee-cord jumping or something you find frightening; in fact, it is better if you recall challenging performance situations when you made the bold choice.

Consider situations when you willfully put yourself in danger of losing something—a competition, an award, a position, or even just your pride. Maybe you volunteered to play the opening solo at a summer festival. Maybe it was during a basketball game, with seconds left on the clock, when you went for it and shot the winning basket. Or you could have volunteered to give a speech.

Next, across from each item on the list of seven events, write out the positive results or rewards that occurred for each event. Seeing your previous demonstrations of courage on paper will serve to remind you of the times when you successfully handled fear in the past.

When you have seven or more brave actions from your past written down, go out and purchase a tangible reminder of getting past your fears. Find something special that you can wear or hang on the wall. It will serve as a symbol of your courage. Every time you see it, you will be reminded of the valiant actions that you took despite the fear that you felt at the time.

Here are the things that I would recommend that you do today or in this step on your journey towards peak functioning:

- Practice basic centering at least five times
- Continue to think optimistically
- Make your self-talk positive
- Write out your fears
- Say your most effective process cues out loud several times
- Say your cues to yourself as you are practicing performing
- Practice mental rehearsal at least three times today
- Keep notes about your mental practice sessions
- Write down three things you are doing to build your willpower
- Write out your courage history with seven brave acts from your past

Friday or Step 5

*N*ow you will learn more about strengthening your courage by confronting your fears and taking meaningful action to get past them. As you will see, you will start by looking for uncomfortable or scary situations in your life where you have the opportunity to exercise your courage. Courage is like a muscle; you build it by using it frequently and gradually increasing the repetitions and level of resistance.

As I mentioned, Olympic champion Greg Louganis had the courage of a warrior. When he was 19, he was competing in Russia. As he says in his book, *Breaking the Surface*: "I was doing a reverse dive pike on the 10-meter platform. And I don't know if it was the soft cushioning on the platform that I wasn't used to, or I just was trying a little too hard to do a perfect dive, but I jumped off the platform, brought my legs up and touched my toes, and saw the sun through my legs. That's the last thing I remember. Apparently, I hit the back of my head solidly on the platform and was knocked unconscious."

Greg landed flat on his back. If it weren't for the extra soft padding on the platform, he probably would have died. He was pulled out of the water and remained unconscious for 20 minutes. They took him to a Soviet hospital. The doctors said that he hadn't fractured his skull, probably due to the padding, but he'd certainly suffered a concussion. He returned home a few days later and within a week or so, he was back on the platform. The World Cup was less than two weeks away, so he got back into practicing. He won.

Four years later, Greg was diving at the World University Games in Canada. He was standing on the 7.5-meter platform waiting for the Russian Sergei Chalibashvili on the 10-meter platform above him to do his dive. Greg said, "I knew he was about to do a reverse three-and-a-half, a very difficult dive. I was the person who had started using the dive in international competition, and my doing it pushed the other divers to try to do it, even if they weren't fully prepared. Sergei and I were the only two divers attempting the reverse three-and-a-half at the World University Games."

Evidently, Sergei had come close to hitting his head on the concrete platform several times in warm-ups and many American coaches and divers, including Greg, were very worried about him. Greg said the following:

> I had an awful feeling that he was going to hit. I turned around and looked away from the pool. I plugged my ears. I pulled my ears with my fingers, and I started humming lightly to myself. I didn't want to see or hear him hit the platform. I didn't see it or hear it, but I felt it. There was a jolt, and the whole tower shook. I looked over the edge of the platform and there he was, facedown, not moving. There was quite a bit of blood in the water, and a few people were in the water already pulling him to the side of the pool. Sergei was unconscious, but still breathing.

Sergei was taken to a hospital. He was in a coma. Greg continues:

> When the diving resumed, we were all still shaken. I still had a job to do, but it was almost impossible to concentrate. My next dive was a back three-and-a-half, which I did fine. But then my final dive of the prelims was the same reverse three-and-a-half

Sergei had attempted. Before I did the dive, I asked my coach permission to jump it out, to push out farther from the platform so there would be more space between my head and the concrete as I passed the platform on the way down. I didn't want to take any chances, so I played it safe and jumped it out. I got 4's and 5's, which wasn't great, but in the finals, I did the dive as I usually did and got 8's.

As usual, Greg won the event.

Courage Log

"Courage mounteth with occasion." William Shakespeare

Like a muscle, if you don't use your courage on a continuing basis, you lose its power, at least temporarily. So, you need to flex it constantly. Take healthy risks in any sort of fear-inducing situation and choose to confront it with boldness. In time, this will become an automatic response for you, so that at the first twinge of worry or apprehension, you respond proactively without a second thought. By continuing to act fearlessly, you will soon come to realize that you are a brave person.

Start recording these important moments in a courage log, where you will continuously keep track of your progress in strengthening your courage. Anytime you take a risk and choose to do something that you would rather not do because of fear or discomfort, enter it in your log along with the end result. Even if the outcome is not totally successful, you win just by taking courageous action.

Like bank deposits into a savings account, you are going to keep a record of each one of your bold actions. Keep track of your brave investments as you gain more power over your fear. Over time, you will accumulate interest. Remember to start out with small acts of bravery to get you in the habit of exercising your courage. Starting today, look for opportunities to strengthen your courage muscles. The risk does not need to be big, and certainly not dangerous; it just needs to be something you would normally avoid because of fear. It does not matter what the fear or discomfort happens to be, only that it prevents you from taking a positive step in the right direction.

Each time in the course of a day when you are presented with a situation in which you could flex your courage muscles, and you choose to take that step, write down what you did. It can be anything. If you're working on your speech, video tape your presentation. If you are a musician, you could put a challenging piece of music on your stand, turn on a recording device, and really go for it! Hold nothing back. Don't worry about mistakes. Have the courage to really let it fly. Learn to triumph over your fear of making mistakes. Once you do, you will create fewer mistakes.

If you are a golfer, you could set up a match and play someone better than you. Put a wager on it if you want to gain more entries for your courage log. Make sure that you play aggressively. Every putt that doesn't go in should be several inches past the hole. Try to reach every par-5 in two or three strokes. You are looking to take healthy risks that are beyond what is comfortable for you. Every time you bravely step over that line past comfort and into fear, it helps strengthen your power.

Playing the Edge

"To play it safe is not to play." Robert Altman

Even when executing the most challenging tasks, there should be a feeling of control over your actions and experience. However, sometimes there isn't that feeling of control, particularly when the activity is challenging your capabilities. In order to reach peak functioning, you need to be willing to play the edge. It is the edge where control is possible but not necessarily guaranteed. You can fall off the edge if you don't use your talent and skills to their full potential.

Playing the edge is what can make what you do exciting, and it is what will take your execution to a higher level. This involves the paradox of control: In order to gain a degree of control, you must be willing to lose control at the edge of your abilities. You can develop real power by trusting in your higher abilities and going for it in situations where there are many variables outside of your control. This can be very exhilarating. It's also essential if you want to perform at the peak of your capabilities.

The idea is to play the edge of your true potential and push the envelope beyond your usual limits and fears or the tendency to play it safe. You need to move past your ego and comfort zone so you can explore your highest capabilities. Challenge yourself and play the edge beyond the line of comfort and fear that stands between you and your very best.

Choose your occasions for playing the edge wisely. Please do not do any physically dangerous things. Do not take on the big risks until you get experience beating some of the lesser ones. It is important that you give yourself full permission to bail at any time. If you feel like it's too much, or that you are in over your head, just walk away from it, without any guilt or second thoughts. You can come back another day. You do not need to explain to anyone. Just don't enter it in your log, any more than your bank account records would indicate that you meant to make a deposit but didn't do it that day.

Whenever you take a step outside of your comfort zone and go for it, enter it in your courage log. The goal is to add at least 14 new entries into your log over the next several weeks. By then you will be in the habit of acting bravely without a second thought, like soldiers are trained to do. That's when you will give yourself a special gift, as a symbolic reminder of your brave acts. It will help you remember your courage and what you did to deserve your reward.

Now it's time for you to take another important step in strengthening your courage, by addressing the very beginning of your activity, with the initial execution of your skills. That's the real moment of truth, right before you start, when fear can hold you back or cause you to be tentative or hesitant, which never works. In order for you to achieve a peak level of functioning, you must learn to get past that fear.

Many people tend to hold back in high pressure situations, especially at the beginning. They develop a "play it safe" reflex or habit that causes them to be cautious and hold back. This double-clutching results in disjointed starts that lack confidence and conviction. You need to be willing to run the risk of failure and making mistakes by developing the essential skill of bravely going for it from the outset. Afterwards, note it as the next entry in your log as you keep strengthening your courage.

These are the things that I would recommend that you do today or during this step:

- Practice basic centering at least 6 times
- Continue to think optimistically
- Keep your self-talk positive
- Practice mental rehearsal at least three times today.
- Write down the things you are doing to build your willpower
- Write out your courage history with another 7 brave acts from your past
- Start your courage log with 3 brave acts today
- Play the edge today with the execution of your skills
- Imagine everything going well tomorrow in your upcoming live event

In the meantime, try to get good rest and sleep. If your performance event is in the morning, you may want to get up a little early. It will allow you time to get your energy up to a positive level, meeting the day with optimism and positive self-talk, expecting to do your best. Before you go to bed, make the commitment that you will go for it tomorrow and let it fly, no matter what. Imagine that.

Week 1

Saturday

*W*elcome to the first live performance event. You can start today whenever you are ready to go, but you only get one shot to execute your skills at the highest level possible. Get yourself centered and in a positive mindset before you start. Imagine an ideal performance from beginning to end. Make sure to summon up your courage and play the edge to make your best happen. Commit to go for it, and then let it fly! Afterwards, take a break before you review the event.

Then, in your journal or notebook evaluate your performance honestly and objectively. Give yourself a rating or score from 1 to 99 (poor to peak) in each of the categories.

Centered _____ ___

Positive mindset _____

Confidence _____

Courage _____

Execution _____

Write out all the things that you did extremely well in your performance. Capture those things in writing, exactly what they looked and sounded like, and what they felt like, when you were executing your skills at your highest levels. Vividly imagine them as they happened during your performance. Make sure that you can see, feel, and hear them being executed correctly in your right brain.

Next, think about the things in your execution that need the most improvements. List them in your journal or notebook. Then prioritize them in the order of what needs the most attention next week. You need to take a hard look at those things, especially with the unforced mistakes that you made. What do you think caused those failures?

Failure

Here are Coach O'Brien's thoughts about failure:

Failing is something almost everyone who has succeeded has tasted at least once. Most of the highly successful athletes and people in other fields that I have known, have experienced failing. In many cases, they hit rock bottom before they could rise from the ashes and eventually succeed. Everybody who has tried to succeed at something has blown it at some point. It is inevitable.

How you react mentally to failing is the key to whether you can use it to your advantage or let it destroy you. If you internalize the feeling of failing by telling yourself you are a failure, then you have put a negative attitude into action. Productivity is minimal when you go down that road and start to feel sorry for yourself. You can become paralyzed. Of course, you are allowed a small amount of time to feel down about the results but keep that time to a minimum and then respond in a positive way. You need to look at failing as an opportunity to learn!

There are two questions you must always ask yourself when faced with failing, "What did I do that I shouldn't have?" and "What I didn't do that I should have?" Find the answers to these two questions and you establish the foundation to learn from failing and to create a plan and model for success. You may suffer failing more than once, but that doesn't mean you are a failure. You just haven't yet properly created the correct model for success. It needs more shaping and developing. Once you get the model right, when an opportunity presents itself, you will be ready to seize it.

I'd suggest that you take some time today to run errands before you resume your training program on Monday. Consider finishing things like the laundry, emails, phone calls, and grocery shopping so they are out of the way during your next week of training. If you do not have a device that plays music and headphones or earbuds, get them today. Listening to music will be an important part of your training program and one of your best allies over the next several weeks.

Music Playlist

"Music produces a kind of pleasure which human nature cannot do without." Confucius

Music can have a significant effect on your state of mind, energy, focus, moods, and level of performance. A fast tempo can cause the brain to resonate with the beat, which raises energy levels and increases alertness and focus. It can facilitate movement and exercise, and it can reduce feelings of physical and mental fatigue. Upbeat tunes and positive lyrics can increase self-confidence and serve as a source of inspiration.

Music has the power to animate people on many different levels. Physically, we tap our feet or fingers to the beat, start dancing, or play air guitar. After a great performance, we say that it felt "moving." Music can transport us to different times or places way outside ourselves or take us deep within.

The right kind of music can change brain activity. One study tested adults' reactions to different types of music with functional magnetic resonance imaging. The MRI monitored their brain activity while they listened to music, and it showed areas of the brain activated by the sounds. The subjects listened to classical, country, rock, rap, Chinese opera, and they chose one additional song or piece that was a personal favorite.

Each type of music they heard activated different areas of the brain, with increased network connections between those areas. However, nothing aroused the subjects' brains as much as when they listened to their favorite music, no matter what it was. Hearing their favorites significantly improved their brain connectivity in the cerebral cortex, both left and right hemispheres, as well as the limbic system and emotion center.

Create a playlist today of your favorite high-energy songs that will get you moving first thing in the morning. Put several of your favorite tunes together that will pump you up and get you psyched to head out on your brisk morning walk or jog. The songs should get you energized and happily going on your way to reach your peak.

Week 2

Monday or Step 6

*W*elcome to your second week or sixth step on your adventure and journey towards your highest levels of functioning. Now you will learn about intermediate centering, routines, starting your morning routine, focus, attention spans, focused attention, and redirecting your attention to the task at hand. This may sound like a lot to take in, but please be patient with yourself and with the process! We'll cover a little bit at a time so you can take it all in.

Let me introduce you to Deborah. She was a practicing attorney for many years and when she retired, she took up competitive ballroom dancing. She brought quite a bit of anxiety to her dance performance, even though she didn't identify herself as a nervous person. She explained, "It's funny, I'm not generally an anxious person. I feel confident when I start a new challenge, or a hobby or new project. And I was a confident lawyer. I'm the parent of five and I'm pretty confident in my real life, but boy, get me on the ballroom dance floor and it's like I'm freaking out."

Deborah recalled the first time that she competed. She had already put in "a lot of time, a lot of energy, a lot of money, a lot of blood, sweat, and tears that go into improving your skills and doing well enough to be able to compete on the floor and not look like an idiot."

But at her first competition, she suddenly felt a lot of anxiety. It was a very big event, she had only been dancing for six months, and it was her first time competing. "I kind of got thrown to the wolves. I had no idea what it was going to be like. I wasn't adequately prepared in any way. I knew my dance steps, but I wasn't emotionally prepared for the stress of the whole thing. For the first and only time in my life, I had an almost complete out-of-body experience. I totally blanked out. It was so traumatizing to have this happen!"

During the experience, she had no idea what was going on and felt terrified. She'd never had an anxiety or panic attack before or since that moment. Deborah started working with me on that and to improve her focus as a way of getting ready for her next big performance. She started doing mental rehearsal and she learned to focus her mind on what was happening right then in the present moment as a way of quieting her left-brain chatter and to settle into what she called her "right-brain happy place."

Deborah worked on mental rehearsal every day as she was getting ready for a performance or competition. For her, that meant imagining in her right brain what the event was going to look like. She thought about "what it was going to feel like when we were on the dance floor, not just practicing the steps, but picturing where the lights would be in the ballroom, what the temperature would be like, what the floor would feel like under my feet as we danced to the rhythm of the music." I encouraged her to vividly imagine all the details of the event from inside and out.

I also taught Deborah basic centering, and after 21 repetitions, she started to learn the intermediate form of centering, as you will start to do today. Deborah also completed the courage history and courage log in her journal, and she began playing the edge whenever she danced. She found all of it very helpful on the dance floor.

Like Deborah, you have been working this past week on your state of mind. By now, I hope that your thoughts are starting to shift from pessimistic and critical to optimistic and positive. They need to be moving from negative outcome thinking and outcome thinking to process thinking or mental quiet. You should be in your right brain when you are executing your skills. As these mental habits change for the better, you can start to make your affirmations more succinct and to the point.

Affirmations

Let's start to reduce the affirmative sentences or phrases down to key words to remind yourself to get centered, be confident, bring your courage, trust in the process, and focus your attention in the here and now. Write these statements in your journal or notebook and say them aloud.

- I'm able to center myself
- I know how to focus
- I'm able to quiet my mind
- I'm very confident
- I'm a courageous person
- I trust myself
- I imagine my best

These affirmations could even be shortened to one-word reminders: Center. Focus. Confidence. Courage. Trust. Say these aloud and in front of a mirror. Ultimately, they could all be captured in one word which should now have special meaning to you, and that word is "center." The only thing better is to imagine it going well in mental quiet, which you can access in your right brain. All you need to do is *imagine* yourself being centered, confident, courageous, and focused in the here and now, doing your best.

Short Affirmations

- Center
- Focus
- Confidence
- Courage
- Focus

Now that you've spent some time reminding yourself of these affirmations, you are ready to learn the intermediate form of centering. The steps are similar, but this form of the centering process has only five steps, takes less time, and is more efficient.

Intermediate Centering

"Happiness is self-generated as the mind becomes still. As we become involved with the desires of the world, we lose that centering, that stillness." Frederick Lenz

Start by finding a comfortable standing position, with your feet shoulder-width apart and a slight bend in the knees. Your back should be straight. Place your hands over your center. Make sure that you feel in balance, with your head either up or down toward your chest. Set your clear intention ahead of time and state it to yourself. In addition, pick your focal point ahead of time. Make sure that it is lower than eye level. After you focus on your point, close your eyes or soften your gaze to a general area on the floor in front of you.

The first step is to focus only on your breathing, for three breaths. Be mindful of your breath as you breathe in slowly through your nose, pause for a moment, and then breathe out slowly through your mouth. Breathe slowly into your center, hold it, and then exhale slowly. Focus only on your breathing.

The second step is to scan your upper body for muscle tension. Breathe in slowly and deeply and then pause to check if your jaw is tight. If it is, just slowly breathe out the tension. Then check your neck and throat and breathe out any tightness you may find there. Next, check your entire upper body and breathe out any remaining tension.

The third step is to be at your center, for three breaths. Breathe into your center and try to get a feel for that place. Get out of your head and into your center.

The fourth step is to vividly imagine yourself accomplishing your activity well for three breaths. See it clearly; feel the correct movements; hear it the way you want it to sound, or fully sense any combination of these, as long as you can do it in three breaths.

The fifth step is to allow the energy to come up from your center, through your body, up and up, until it reaches your eyes. Then focus your attention back on your point. You are now centered and ready to perform your best.

Create a practice log in your journal or notebook, and practice intermediate centering twice today and then even more times every day, just like last week. Once again, set up a token economy and reward to motivate. When you've practiced it at least 21 times, you will receive a reward as a symbol of your efforts. Then you will be ready for the advanced form of centering next week.

Intermediate Centering

1. **Start abdominal breathing.** Breathe slowly and deeply three times into your center.
2. **Scan and release muscle tension.** Check for tightness, then breathe it out.
3. **Be at your center.** Get out of your head and into your center for three breaths.
4. **Imagine it correctly.** See it, feel it, hear it the way you intend.
5. **Direct your energy to your point.** Let the energy flow from your center out to your focus point.

It is time to start developing your daily and weekly routines. Physical routines involve patterns of sleep, rest, exercise, and recovery. Mental routines involve centering, focusing attention, and listening to the appropriate music. Emotional routines involve strategies for coping with high stress levels while strengthening your bravery, with daily entries in your Courage Log. Your weekly routines will involve these activities six days a week, with one day off.

The goal of the physical routine is for you to go into the final event feeling fresh and rested, with lots of good energy, and in a great mood. You need to be able to handle all the stress along the way and be ready to courageously execute your skills, no matter what, in your final performance. In the meantime, it will help to eat whatever you consider to be healthy and drink more water. Try to reduce or eliminate alcohol, caffeine, and sugary drinks.

Morning Routine

"He who is outside the door has already a good part of the journey behind him." Dutch proverb

> Even after you have chosen an endeavor for which you have a passion, there will still be days you just don't feel like pursuing it. You may wake up in the morning and just won't feel like doing what you know should be done. You must make a choice. If you don't get up and do what you need to do, you are losing time, you're unproductive and you are negatively affecting your ability to reach your potential. Only you can make the choice. You need to learn to make yourself go and do the best you can for that day.
>
> Coach O'Brien

At the least, you need to be in decent physical shape to perform your very best in several weeks. A good morning routine will kick start your day and set you up to do your best. The ritual will quickly get your energy flowing after you wake up, make your body more supple, and put you in a good mood. You can do a trial run of your new morning routine tomorrow.

Mia found the morning routine to be particularly helpful. Mia was in music school, and as a student, she didn't really have a particular daily routine she needed to follow. She'd come a long way from the original panic attack that put us in touch; centering, focus, and cue utilization had all helped her progress towards confidence, but she still didn't feel it every day.

She had come to me with a very negative self-image, and that was still her baseline assumption about herself. Confidence in herself had started to develop, but irregularly. She said, "I was getting frustrated because I could see when it worked and I could see the progression, but it wasn't consistent enough."

I asked her, "What do you do every day? What do you do outside?" Being a student, and one struggling with her mental health, she responded, "Well, it depends on the day, you know? I don't really have a set thing because rehearsals and lessons—they change week to week. She even had days where her mind wouldn't let her get out of bed, wouldn't let her get something to eat, because she felt so down about herself. I wanted her to find that confidence again and have it be a regular part of her life, so we started talking about a morning routine.

We started building her morning routine around her partner's schedule. He had a regular nine-to-five job, so we decided she would create a schedule to mirror that. The first thing she would do is drink water every morning and go to school, even if she didn't practice when she got there. She knew her new schedule was to drink water first thing and leave the house by 8:30.

The next week, we added in more points on her schedule, like practice time and time off. She started practicing three or four hours every day, according to her new schedule, and it all started with the morning routine. "That was a huge, huge thing," Mia recalls, "I have days where it doesn't always go to plan, but it's switched over now. Now my confidence is the regular thing, and I have some irregular not-so-good days, whereas before it was completely the other way around."

So, how do you get to a point where the morning routine is part of your new normal? If you're like Mia, you may need some extra inducement to help you get going, which is why I suggest you set up the token economy and reward (like you have done for centering) for starting and following through on the morning routine. Thoughtfully consider what your tokens will be, specifically what you need to do to earn them and exactly what that reward will be. Hopefully by now you have learned how effective a desired reward can be for changing your willingness to do something that you would rather not do, like basic centering or the morning routine.

Here's what the morning routine looks like. For your first day, you will need to get up about 10 minutes early. Turn on your playlist of energizing music. As soon as possible, drink at least 8 oz of water to gear up your body's metabolism. Within a few minutes, splash cold water vigorously in your face at least seven times. This will shock your nervous system and release adrenaline into your bloodstream. That will wake you up right away. Or you can take a short, cool (not cold) shower. The discomfort will release endorphins, which will make you feel better, especially after you turn the water off.

Get outside within a few minutes, before you have time to talk yourself out of it. If the weather is really bad, you can do the first part of the routine indoors. Get your body supple by stretching slowly, and then increase your heart rate by about 20% by climbing stairs, doing jumping jacks, or jogging in place.

However, it is better to start by going outside. The fresh air and direct natural light will signal your body and brain that it is time to wake up. Stretch slowly and then take a brisk walk, bike, or jog for at least five minutes. As you do, breathe deeply. If you would like to take a longer walk or jog, please do so. After you return, sit down and get yourself centered in the here and now.

Morning Routine Checklist:

- ✓ Wake up to energizing music
- ✓ Drink 8 oz water
- ✓ Splash cold water on your face 7 times
- ✓ Get outside within minutes
- ✓ Stretch and walk or jog briskly
- ✓ Center after you get home

After you center, check centering off of your list, as well as the rest of the completed activities of your morning routine. Checklists were proven to increase the effectiveness of B-17 pilots in the second world war. They are used by surgeons in operating rooms and NASA engineers before launching spacecraft.

Checklists reduce human error, save time, and ensure that everything is done correctly. It feels good to check things off that you have accomplished, especially early in the day. The morning routine is a highly effective way to strengthen your willpower, which will come in handy later in your adventure. Taking your first steps with your morning routine marks the beginning of stage 6 with new conditions on your hero's journey.

Your new morning routine is a very important part of your training. So, like the Nike commercial says, "just do it." No excuses. It's not *that* hard. And it only takes about 10 minutes or so. The toughest steps are the first ones you choose to take. It won't take long before you realize how effective it can be in the morning. It will get you off to an energized start and put you in the right frame of mind and a positive emotional state every day on your journey.

As it was for Mia, the morning routine was a significant aspect of the training for both Deborah and Alexa. Alexa was able to fit the morning routine into a practice of morning quiet time she already included in her life, but it takes a few days to get into the routine and start realizing its many benefits. To help you get there, remember to use your token economy, and give yourself a star, checkmark, or other reminder of completing your morning routines on the way to a nice reward.

Below are excerpts from Coach O'Brien's article about the work ethic necessary for success in any serious endeavor:

> Consistent hard work, not just three or four days a week, but every day is the key to opening the door to reach your potential. A "do whatever it takes" attitude is necessary. Effort, determination, and persistence are as important as

performance. Persistence pays off! Do more than you think you can. When moving from one phase of life to another, we need to use the qualities and good habits formed in the previous challenge into the next one.

Most people have not yet reached their work limit. People who say they are now giving 120% (which is impossible) are really acknowledging that they used to think they were giving 100%, but in reality, they were working well below that level. Keep challenging yourself to do more! Show up every day, even when you don't feel well, be there and do what you can. Of course, there will be days when that isn't possible, but developing the attitude that, except in dire circumstances, you will be there to do your best means there will be far fewer missed days and more opportunities to improve.

One way to improve your work efficiency is to prioritize your workday. If there is something or some things that you are dreading having to do, do them first, then take on the easier tasks. You will tackle the hardest jobs when you are mentally fresh and full of energy and the distracting thought of that thing you dread doing will not be in the back of your mind and negatively affect everything else you do.

Focus

"Nothing interferes with my concentration. You could put an orgy on in my office and I would not look up. Well, maybe once." Isaac Asimo

After starting your morning routine, it helps to be able to focus throughout the day. Let's learn more about concentration and focus. Although Deborah may have known very well how to concentrate in her left brain as an attorney, her left brain was not helping her or her dance partner. In order for her to execute at her best, especially in major competitions, she would need to learn about focus and practice it, both on and off the dance floor.

Learning about focus involves four distinct levels of concentration involved in executing highly complex, coordinated movement skills, especially under stress:

1. Awareness
2. Attention
3. Concentration
4. One-Pointed Concentration (OPC)

Focus

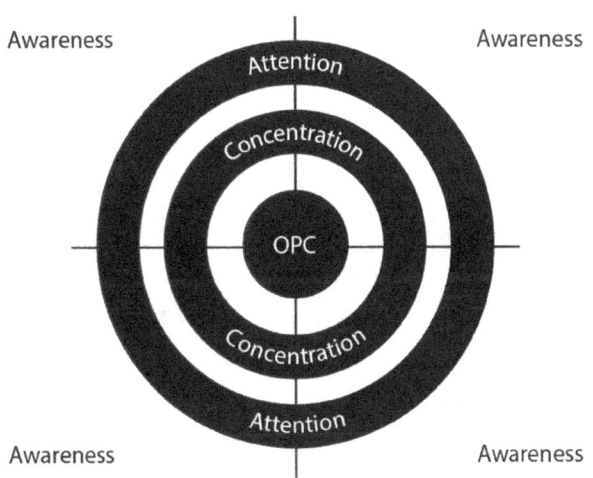

The outermost ring, where the image indicates "awareness," is your conscious awareness. Awareness is your current knowledge of your immediate surroundings as well as whatever you may be perceiving internally. This information comes from your senses, emotions, body, and mind. This awareness allows you to integrate information from the environment with your thoughts, feelings, perceptions, and physical sensations.

Basic awareness will help you control your actions and satisfy the immediate demands of the performance. Awareness of external things can be a source of distractions, but higher levels of awareness involve being aware of yourself as well as being aware of your awareness itself. These higher levels of conscious awareness are attained by actively monitoring your perceptions, sensations, thoughts, and emotions, as well as your actions, without judgment.

The next inner ring of the target is attention. Attention means focused awareness on just one thing, to the exclusion of everything inside and outside your body and mind that is continually competing for your attention. When your wide beam of awareness is narrowed on just one object or process, you start to pay attention. It is difficult to sustain attention on any one thing or process for any amount of time without proper training and practice.

There are numerous sources of distraction that can keep us from focusing our full attention on any one object. We live in a continual state of partial attention, split focus, and inattention caused by ever-changing events and incoming information. We experience endless waves of external stimuli, accompanied by incessant thoughts, a range of emotions, modulating sounds, varying shapes, colors, tastes, textures, smells, and sensations. Our attention gets divided as the mind drifts out of focus or simply wanders away.

When the mind wanders, the distracting thoughts are mostly about the ego or "me." Me-thoughts are those that recount *my* history and narrate *my* story while pondering *my* current situation. This is the cognitive default zone, known in neuroscience as the "default mode network," and it's where the mind tends to drift when it is not actively engaged in a challenging task requiring directed attention. Performing a challenging task can shut off the "me" distractions, at least temporarily. Without the need to focus on any one thing, the mind slips into the default mode, and we zone out for seconds or even minutes at a time, often without even realizing it.

Attention Span

"I have an extraordinary attention span...if I have a gift, that's probably the best gift that's given me." Paul Newman

Let's start with the basics. It begins, of course, in childhood. Children start to develop their attention and ego when they are toddlers. They learn to recognize individuals and recognize themselves as separate from others, and they claim things as their own. They can also focus on single objects, especially if they are moving, shiny, or unique. However, toddlers have a very limited attention span and are easily distracted by more interesting objects, sounds, or their own physical sensations, like hunger, pain, or needing to be held or entertained.

Although toddlers have a short attention span, most adults do not fare much better. Attention is a very limited and temporary resource that can be negatively affected by an endless variety of influences: people, stress, fatigue, anxiety, arousal, noise, movement, changes, disinterest, cognitive preoccupation, or emotional turmoil. Our adult minds are constantly bombarded by an ongoing stream of thoughts, sensory perceptions, feelings, and incoming technical data, advertising, and messages. No wonder it can feel like our attention spans are not much longer than those of toddlers!

Imagine babysitting an active toddler, maybe 2 or 3 years old. Picture yourself trying to get the child to stay within a three-foot circle, drawn in chalk on the floor. Although you instruct him or her to stay there, that's unlikely to happen for more than a few seconds at most. Once the toddler is out of the circle, you can make it better or worse. Yelling at the child for not staying in the circle will cause the child to run away or have a similar negative reaction, with even less time spent in the circle.

If you are in the habit of criticizing yourself for not paying attention or for making mistakes, it's like yelling at a toddler to concentrate. It just makes matters worse. You'll move farther away from your point in the center of your circle. If you want the toddler to spend more time within the circle, you need to gently guide them back into the circle when you see them leave. And you do it again the next time they leave.

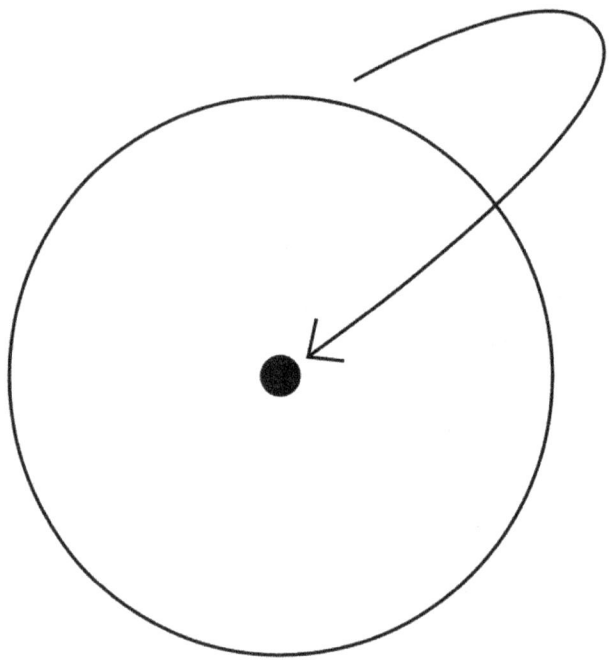

Focused Attention

"Ninety percent of my game is mental. It's my concentration that has gotten me this far." Chris Evert

For most people, focused moments don't last very long. There are countless things that can pull you out of your circle and cause you to be out of focus. You need to fight to keep your focused attention on point within the hypothetical circle. I use the term "fight" intentionally; it can be a real battle to keep your mind on the immediate task at hand in challenging circumstances for more than a few moments. But that's what's required for you to do your best.

As you'll soon realize, whenever the mind is fully engaged in a task that requires willful and undivided attention, there is a constant and opposing force trying to pull it away from the job. This struggle causes the mind to wander away from the required effort and meander into casual rumination, worries, and aimless thoughts about "me." This is where the mind usually goes when it's not engaged in tasks that require focused attention.

The wandering generates distracting background noise and causes free-floating anxiety. It leads to zoning out as the brain's default mode. Mulling things over in passive awareness opens the door for your mind to go to other places. Once it leaves, your focus can be gone for seconds or even minutes before you may notice. Catching a mind that has wandered is not easy, especially after you get caught up in thoughts, worries, or fantasies, and especially if those thoughts, worries, or fantasies have to do with possible negative outcomes for your upcoming performance or event.

However, you can train your mind to catch the drift sooner, so you can bring your focus back to your point faster and spend more time focused within your circle of concentration. As soon as you catch your mind focusing somewhere else or on something else, just guide your focus back inside your circle and back on point. As soon as you are aware that you are zoning out, say, "center," or "focus," to yourself. Then focus your attention exclusively on the task at hand. Learn to do this without any fuss, fanfare, judgment, or other unnecessary delays. Just get back on task as soon as possible.

Attentional control training consists of noticing when your mind wanders, then bringing it back on point and staying there until it leaves again, then bringing it back on point again, again and again. This is the same process used in awareness meditation and it's also like how Olympic athletes approach strength training in the weight room, where they execute countless repetitions to build their muscles and power.

Focus Exercise 1: Redirecting Attention

For this exercise, you need to choose what your specific focus will be, and it should be only one thing. It could be your breath, any one thought or idea, an object, sensation, sound, feeling, or single image. It doesn't really matter what it is. It's the process of willfully attending to just one thing, like your breath, that's most important. You'll soon realize how active your mind can become, especially when you're trying to control it or keep it from wandering.

You may have heard about this practice as a type of meditation before. In fact, it is often referred to as mindfulness meditation, or awareness of breathing meditation. It is a very powerful method for developing your powers of attention and improving your ability to focus, and it can also help to calm an overly anxious mind.

As you practice, stay focused on the one thing, like your breath, until your attention strays. Then bring it back to what you have chosen to focus on, without any delay. Repeat the process again and again. Whether it is a muscle or your focus, repetition builds power and endurance. Attention training will strengthen your focus so you can keep your attention on the task at hand for longer and longer periods. Practice this attentional exercise today and as part of your morning routine tomorrow. Keep track of your repetitions, insights, and progress with focus in your journal or notebook.

Here are the things that I would recommend that you do today or during this step in your continuing journey towards peak functioning:

- Practice Intermediate centering at least 2 times
- Continue your courage log with 3 brave acts
- Consider your worst execution mistakes from your live performance
- Reread Coach O'Brien's ideas about failures
- Write out what you did or didn't do that caused them
- Practice the focus exercise redirecting your attention 3 times
- Review Coach O'Brien's thoughts about the work ethic
- Write down all the things you are doing to build your willpower
- Plan on starting your morning routine tomorrow

Week 2:

Tuesday or Step 7

"Do not shorten the morning by getting up late; look upon it as the quintessence of life, and to a certain extent, sacred." Arthur Schopenhauer

Morning Routine:

✓ Wake up to energizing music

✓ Drink 8 oz water

✓ Splash cold water on your face 7 times

✓ Get outside within minutes

✓ Stretch and walk, bike or jog briskly

✓ Center after you get back home

Now you will be learning more about focus and practicing it. We will discuss perfectionism, striving for excellence, the value of humor and laughter, psychology and the mind, early pioneers in the field of psychology, the Freudian model, ego defense mechanisms, and a focusing exercise for accepting reality. Hopefully, you have already done your morning routine for the first time. If so, congratulations! Make sure that you give yourself one token for your efforts getting past inertia. The first steps in any venture are often the most challenging.

My next client whom I'd like you to meet is Bart. He is a brass player who was in his 20's playing with the National Symphony in Poland. He first contacted me in 2002, when he had several important auditions coming up in Europe in just a matter of months. As we worked together, we discovered that he was very left-brain dominant, with a tendency to overthink everything. He was very motivated to win an audition and get a full-time job. He was very serious—too serious— and highly perfectionistic.

Fortunately, Bart was also bright and enthusiastic about improving his mental game. He had high scores on his assessments in courage and mental toughness, which likely came from his background in the martial arts with karate and aikido. However, he had not been playing well for quite a while. He tended to doubt his abilities, despite his past hard work and countless hours of practice. Now Bart needed to develop his imaginative right brain and especially his sense of humor.

We'll talk more about humor in a bit, but one idea that had a big impact on Bart was the simple idea to smile before playing his instrument. He recalls, "Dr. Greene said I should smile each and every time before I bring up my horn to play. I should just feel the emotion of the piece, then smile and play what I'm feeling." After he started to smile more, Bart noticed that smiling also improved the blood circulation in his face. This gave him a more relaxed embouchure and made it easier for him to play. It also brought more positive emotion to the music! This definitely helped, but in order to ever reach peak functioning with his playing, Bart really needed to learn how to be less of a perfectionist.

Perfectionism

"Even if the world were perfect, it wouldn't be." Yogi Berra

Perfectionism is a definite impediment to peak functioning. Just like so many people I've worked with, including Mia, Alexa, Jacqueline and Deborah, Bart was a perfectionist. At one time in the distant past, so was

Greg Louganis. He, too, had struggled with perfectionism, until the 1982 World Championships in Ecuador. As he worked on his ten-meter dive, he realized then that, "perfection is something to strive for, but it's never obtainable."

Greg had his biggest lesson about this when he did his inward one-and-a-half in pike. "I got straight ten's. Ten is supposed to be perfect and I thought, 'Oh my God,' because then I started thinking they're going to expect tens on all the rest of my dives, because I just got tens on this one. My next dive was easy, but it didn't go all that great, because I was so hung up on the perfection thing. So, I decided to shake that off and say, time to go to work. Focus on each dive because really each dive is a new creation."

Greg had realized that each dive is its own unique creation. He could come back to the pool two hours later and do the same dive, but that next time, he might not get all tens. He learned early on that "there is no such thing as perfect and to be content and appreciative of what you're able to create in that moment in time in that space of less than 3 seconds." He thought about all the dives that occurred over the course of that competition. That time, there were 11 dives on the three-meter and 10 dives on the platform. If he made the preliminaries and finals on both, that would be 22 dives on springboard and 20 dives on 10 platforms, or "42 opportunities to practice peak performance, not perfection, and strive for excellence."

Jacqueline, the bassoonist, also came to a series of her own realizations about perfectionism. She said, "perfectionism usually happens with all musicians, but especially double reed players. We have to make part of our instrument every day. We have to adjust and make the reed, and it's really easy to spend way more time doing that than practicing, because we're always looking "for the perfect reed and it doesn't exist, but we're always trying to make it and to get it. It's really hard to put the reed knife down and start practicing. We can easily spend two-thirds of our time making reeds. Sometimes more. Sometimes you have to just say to yourself, okay, that's as far as I can go, I'm going to practice. I still don't like the reeds I made, but I have to practice.

She explained that for an audition, you need to make even more reeds, so that you'll have choices on hand for any weather changes. If it's humid, dry, cold, or warm, this all can affect the reeds: "They're constantly changing because they are made of organic living material." Because of this, we worked on not needing to be perfect and accepting both herself and her reeds as they were, because they were never going to be perfect.

If you are a perfectionist or have perfectionistic tendencies like some of my clients, you probably set extremely high standards for yourself. You likely believe that you should always perform up to that high mark, even under less-than-ideal circumstances. This goal can push you to try to perform flawlessly, but it can also prevent that from happening. Perfectionism is an unrealistic expectation. It can become a serious impediment to achieving a peak performance.

If you set your goals unrealistically high and demand of yourself that you achieve perfection, you will set yourself up for failure and disappointment. You will realize that you are not able to complete the intended task perfectly, on schedule, to everyone's approval. If you expect to be perfect, you will eventually realize that no matter what you do, you will most likely never reach perfection, and this can feel so demoralizing.

Perfectionists get caught up in their left brains, making them concerned with small parts, technical details, and precision. The left brain thinks in two dimensions: yes or no, black or white. It causes rigidity in decision-making, self-critical judgments, and a lack of meaningful action. Trying to be perfect will limit your performance. Perfectionism makes people cautious, in order to minimize the possibility of error, but caution will actually increase the likelihood of making mistakes.

If you are interested in doing your best rather than trying to be perfect, there is a way to get there. It involves a shift from the left brain to the right and striving for excellence rather than perfection. Focus on doing your best with continuous improvement, because this *is* under your control, instead of trying to be perfect, which is out of your control.

As you work on this, you can also make better use of your right brain. The right brain is the brain's creative side, it is able to perceive in three or more dimensions: yes, no, and maybe; black, white, or even all the colors of the rainbow. Only the right brain can see images of flowing movements, hear beautiful music, and feel physical motions without actually moving, like during mental rehearsals.

The right brain is also able to conceive a spectrum of future possibilities. It can anticipate contingencies and help create desired events. Keep your right brain engaged in the process, not the outcome, as you focus on doing your best in the moment. The solution to perfectionism is to continually strive for excellence, not perfection.

Striving for Excellence

"Striving for perfection is the greatest stopper there is. You'll be afraid you can't achieve it… It's your excuse for not doing anything. Instead, strive for excellence, doing your best." Sir Laurence Olivier

Striving for excellence is how you can reach a high level of self-confidence. It means doing the best you can daily, in a never-ending quest for improvement. Every day, try to do just a little better than you did on the previous days. By doing this, beyond any doubt you will achieve unconditional trust in yourself and your abilities. Strive for excellence, not for perfection, every day, continuing to surpass what you have already accomplished in the days before.

Today or during this step, I highly recommend that you:

- Practice self-forgiveness
- Acknowledge that you are human
- Learn to accept your perfectionistic tendencies without giving in to them
- Try to not try so hard
- Set high standards, not unattainable goals

- Be grateful for your opportunities to fail on the way to freedom and success

- There is no real failure, other than not trying your best

- Continually strive for excellence

In your journal or notebook, write out your action plan of how you will move past your perfectionistic tendencies over the next few weeks. You will pursue excellence as you prepare for your upcoming performances. Use your creative right brain to vividly imagine your ideal performances. Tomorrow, journal or notebook about striving for excellence in your morning routine

Humor and Fun

"Optimism and humor are the grease and glue of life. Without both of them we would never have survived our captivity." Philip Butler, former Vietnam POW

In addition to moving past their perfectionism, both Jacqueline and Bart needed to work less and play more, meaning have more fun! Rather than working on reeds or musical repertoire, they needed to play music and have fun while doing it. Happy musicians sound better and tend to perform better under pressure. Because of their upcoming events, they both needed to learn this valuable lesson as soon as possible.

Greg Louganis shares this great story about humor:

> I remember that before my first World Championships in Berlin I was with my coach Ron O'Brien. He had a barbecue at his house months before. And we were chatting about the times when I performed well. He said, "when you perform well, you're smiling, you're happy, you're dancing around and all that". I said, "well Ron, if you don't see me having fun, then you have my full-on permission to kick me in the ass."

And so, months later, I was in Berlin. I was really nervous because this was my first big international meet after the '76 Olympic games. And I was a silver medalist…There was also a lot of other stuff that was going on in my life, and the weather was bad. It was cold and kind of drizzly. I'm a fair-weather diver. I'm a California guy. I love the sun and warmth.

I was miserable and in such a bad mood. I remember being in the hot shower, that was the only way we could keep warm. So I was under the hot shower, and then I feel this kick in the butt and then I see Ron walking away from me. I'm thinking in my head thinking, oh my God, I know I'm diving bad, but you know, it's come to you know, physical abuse. That put me in an even worse mood.

Then I got on an elevator to go up to the 10-meter platform. On the way up, I remembered that I had told him to kick me in the butt if I wasn't having fun. I started laughing, and then I got off the elevator and I looked down at Ron and smiled as if to say, watch this Coach. I did my front three and a half somersaults in pike, and I nailed the dive I missed in Montreal. It was my first World Championship gold medal on 10-meter.

It was just finding humor in those situations that really alleviates a lot of that fear, that pressure, and converts that into a more positive way. And it also just drops the tension out of the body. And like, it brings you back to your presence of mind. Yeah, it's serious, but it's not that serious. You know what I say, it's too important to take too seriously. There needs to be a lightness to it.

Greg never lost a major competition ever again after he started with Ron.

Laughter

"A day without laughter is a day wasted." Charlie Chaplin

Keeping your sense of humor, and especially being able to laugh out loud, can be of immense help to anyone who needs to function effectively under pressure. Norman Cousins was the editor-in-chief of the *Saturday Review* for more than 30 years. In 1964, when Cousins was 49, he was diagnosed with a rare form of arthritis and collagen disease. This disease aggressively attacked the connective tissue in the spine, causing severe, chronic pain. Conventional treatments included spinal surgery and heavy pain medication. These approaches offered some relief from the extreme pain and kept the condition from worsening, but there was no real cure.

Doctors told Cousins that he had a one in five-hundred chance of improving, so he should get his affairs in order. Soon after receiving the final diagnosis, he checked himself out of the hospital against doctor's orders. He stopped taking his medications, including the 38 aspirins and injections of Phenylbutazone (a horse tranquilizer) that he had received daily at the hospital. He vowed to fight the disease with confidence and humor. His recovery plan included large doses of Vitamin C, an optimistic attitude, positive emotions, and daily laughter.

Cousins bought a movie projector and a pile of comedy movies, like the Marx Brothers, Laurel and Hardy, and funny TV programs like *Candid Camera*. He spent a lot of time at home laughing, sometimes until his stomach hurt. Cousins also read humorous books, and he soon found that ten minutes of induced, hearty laughter could give him two hours of uninterrupted, deep sleep without any pain.

Cousins eventually made a near-full recovery from his "incurable disease." In 1979, he wrote a book about his experiences with healing using laughter. He established a department at the UCLA Medical School to investigate the connection between healing and humor. He died at 75 from heart failure, 26 years after the initial diagnosis of his spinal condition. He said, "Of all the gifts bestowed on human beings, hearty laughter must be close to the top."

In 1995, Dr. Madan Kataria developed Laughter Yoga to help patients heal from a variety of disorders. The practice involves creating laughter by doing a series of exercises with fellow chucklers. Deliberate laughter is part of their daily routine. Dr. Kataria found even fake laughter has healing power, but honest belly laughter is better.

Figure out what will make you laugh out loud for several minutes every day. Look for late night TV monologues, or watch funny videos on YouTube, cable, Netflix, Facebook, Instagram, or other online media. Find and use whatever it takes to make you laugh out loud for a good while. This laughter will definitely help you deal with the increasing stress you'll be facing in the coming weeks.

Psychology and the Mind

While laughter will get you to a better mindset, you'll also be able to move forward on your journey by learning more about what goes on in your brain and in your mind. For that reason, we turn now to two early pioneers who explored the previously uncharted territory of psychology and the mind: William James and Sigmund Freud. Later, we'll look at the equally important work of Carl Gustav Jung. Each of these pioneers developed their own unique model or map of the mind or human psyche. Although their theoretical constructs of the mind each have their differences, all the models are relevant to understanding concentration, unforced errors, and the different components of peak functioning.

William James was the first professor to teach a course in psychology at Harvard in 1875. He lectured and wrote about the mind, the ego, focused attention, willpower, mysticism, peak experiences, and human consciousness. Consciousness refers to our continual awareness of the external environment, as well as our own individual history, impressions, thoughts, physical sensations, imaginings, and feelings.

The major characteristic of consciousness that James recognized is its very personal nature. Thoughts are either "my thoughts" or "your thoughts". They are the result of our personal states of mind that separate each of us from everyone else. This sense of "me-ness" (of individual identity) is what James called pure ego. Pure ego gives each of us a unique perception of reality. Our unique and personal identification with our own stream of thoughts and feelings confirms our separateness from everyone else.

William James' theory of willpower, or volition, involves the process in the mind that directs voluntary movements towards a desired result. Bringing any thought into reality depends upon a person's knowledge, experience, confidence, willingness, energy, and degree of applied effort.

The term willpower had not been used prior to the 1850s, but it has since become a common term referring to the force needed to "will" something into being. The word *will* in this sense is related to the Old English word *willian*, meaning "to determine by act of choice," as in a last will and testament. Thankfully, you are not facing your last will and testament, and the only thing you need to will into being is your own continued improvement.

The Freudian Model

"The ego represents what may be called reason and common sense, in contrast to the id, which contains the passions." Sigmund Freud

In Austria in the late 1800's, Sigmund Freud, a physician, developed his own theories at around the same time William James was working on his. Freud was not very interested in James' ideas, especially about consciousness, attention, or willpower. Instead, Freud was focused on sex and its implications for human functioning, as well as his own structure of the mind. Freud's model of the mind contains the id, the ego, and the superego. The Freudian concept of the ego can be thought of as each person's sense of self, or consciousness of one's individual identity. Your ego includes your personal history with memories of all the significant events that you've ever experienced in your life.

Freudian Model

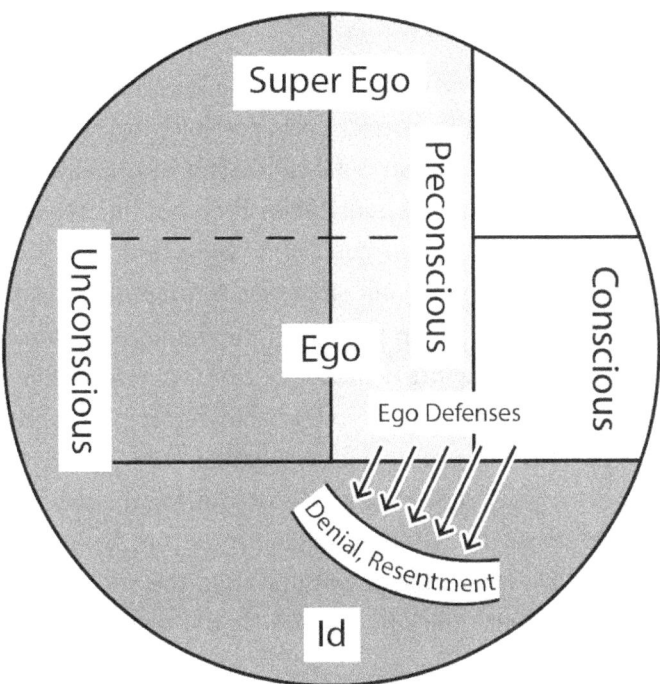

According to Freud, the id is the source of our basic instinctual urges and impulses. This part of our minds contains the libido, which is our passion (including sexual passion), and its never-ending desire for the fulfillment of bodily wants and instant gratification. Freud described this part of the mental structure as a "cauldron of seething excitations." The id acts without thinking and follows the Pleasure Principle: avoid all pain and maximize all pleasure. (You can probably imagine, already, how the id might get in the way of your progress toward a peak performance).

On the other hand, the superego is very concerned with right and wrong, parental norms, social values, cultural mores, and proper behavior. The superego is our conscience. When we were born, we were all pure id. It took many years for the superego to develop, which it did through the teaching of our parents, educators, religious leaders, and coaches. These role models passed on their values and society's rules—many of which run directly contrary to the id's passions and desires.

The superego always aims for impeccable conduct and perfect behavior. Even though this is not really possible, the superego tries to keep the id's drives, wants, and fantasies from happening in reality. The superego uses the language of "should's" and "thou shalt nots" to influence the id's actions. When that fails to prevent the misbehavior, the superego punishes the id with guilt or shame. Neither is helpful to the ego.

The ego mediates between the desires of the id, the admonitions of the superego, and the ongoing demands of external reality. The ego is the only part of Freud's model that is in contact with the real world, and it's also the one that manages all this inner conflict. The ego needs to make judgments and critical decisions; it is also organizing mental material and synthesizing information. The ego plans events and keeps track of the passage of time. In order to cope with all that, the ego needs to have a way of protecting itself. The ego protects itself with what are called ego defense mechanisms.

Ego defense mechanisms include processes such as denial, rationalization, and resentment. Despite these terms having negative connotations in our culture, they are natural and normal. They can even be helpful, warding off recurrent or unpleasant thoughts, bad memories, and unwelcome urges. They relieve anxiety, at least temporarily. However, these mechanisms can cause problems. They can distort reality in a vain attempt to resist what is happening, which can make it difficult to focus one's attention on the task at hand in the here and now.

You can get past the ego's distortion and distraction through nonresistance, or the immediate and unconditional acceptance of whatever is presenting itself to your awareness, just the way it is. The ego sometimes tries to take control, resist, and say no to the changing internal or external events in your present reality. As a result, the ego's efforts will have a detrimental effect on your ability to focus.

You have now learned about James's pure ego and the aspect of consciousness that separates your thoughts from everyone else's. You've also learned about Freud's ego, id, and superego, and how the ego mediates between the competing demands of the conscience-centered superego and the libido-filled id. This information can help you understand what's going on when you are trying to focus on the task at hand. One focusing technique that will come particularly in handy is learning to accept reality and say yes to whatever's going on in the here and now.

Focus Exercise 2: Accepting Reality

"Like the physical, the psychic is not necessarily in reality what it appears to us to be." Sigmund Freud

For this next focusing exercise, you will practice saying yes to whatever may be happening in the present moment around you. You don't have to do anything, other than consciously allow the present moment to be the way it already is. Totally accept each moment just as it is, right here and right now, without judgment. The word yes takes you into reality, wherever you are. When you say yes to the present moment, you can fully embrace the current situation and focus on the task at hand in the here and now. Practice this exercise today, throughout the day, and as part of your morning routine tomorrow. Notice how it helps you to focus. Record your repetitions and thoughts about it in your journal or notebook.

Tomorrow, as part of your morning routine, you will introduce the practice of mindful awareness, sometimes known as insight meditation (or *vipassana* in Sanskrit). The key element in the process is being intensely aware of whatever you happen to be experiencing without getting caught up in it, whether that is a thought, a feeling, or anything else. This practice of awareness means tuning in to and totally accepting yourself and your current conditions, without getting attached to anything other than what happens to be going on in the present moment, wherever you are.

It also is about paying willful attention on purpose in the present moment to things going on outside of you and inside you. That means not paying any further attention to any one thought, emotion, sensation, or sound after you have become aware of it. It includes not following the storyline of your own mental melodrama or memories. If a thought about a potential solution to a problem arises, recognize the thought, but then let your mind move on to something else. When you realize that you are engaged in any of these mental activities, simply go back to being mindful in the here and now.

After you have returned home and centered, take three minutes to focus on your personal experience of your body, mind, and emotions as well as your experience of sensations coming from your external reality. Mindfulness is about letting go any judgments about or attachments to the present moment. The practice involves maintaining active, moment-to-moment awareness of passing thoughts, bodily sensations, emotions, and your immediate, surrounding environment, without fixating on any of them.

Focus all your awareness on everything that you're experiencing in the continuing moment inside you and around you, without becoming attached or fixated on any part of it. When you realize that your attention has been captured by something, whatever it is, just let it go. Bring your awareness back into the here and now without judgment on what's currently happening in the moment, as you let that go in the next moment.

In Focus Exercise 1, you worked on keeping the focus on one thing, like the breath, and returning to this when the attention wanders. This mindfulness activity is a little different. It asks you to be nonjudgmental and aware of whatever is in your circle of awareness at that present moment. Be aware of your breath, thoughts, physical sensations, and sensory input from the external world, like sights, sounds or the temperature of the air. Let your awareness naturally drift to something else, such as a thought or emotional feeling. Don't judge what's happening; simply pay attention to all these things and how they change, for three minutes. This practice emphasizes the development of acceptance of the present moment.

Starting tomorrow, make mindfulness practice a part of your daily routine. Within a week you will notice a significant increase in your ability to be aware of what you're focusing on, when your focus has drifted away from your desired intention, and then be able to keep your mind focused in the here and now for longer and longer periods.

Find time during the day today or during this step, to make sure that you:

- Practice Intermediate centering at least 3 times
- Continue your courage log, including adding 3 brave acts
- Make notes about your perfectionistic tendencies
- Write out your plan for getting past perfectionism
- Find three sources of humor that make you laugh out loud
- Say your short affirmations to yourself before executing your skills
- Practice the Focusing Exercise 2 redirecting your attention 3 times
- Write down all the things you are doing to build your willpower
- Write out five things you can do to strive for excellence
- Commit to following your morning routine starting tomorrow

Week 2

Wednesday or Step 8

"Put yourself in competition with yourself each day. Each morning look back upon your work yesterday and then try to beat it." Charles M. Shelton

Today you will learn even more about the skill of concentration, as you continue practicing it and following your new morning routine. You will find it very helpful once you get used to it. We will also be addressing your ego and how to move beyond its distractions by focusing it in the present moment. We will also be discussing how to create successful events with the power of your mind.

Morning Routine:

✓ Wake up to energizing music

✓ Drink 8 oz water

✓ Splash cold water on your face at least 7 times

✓ Get outside within minutes

✓ Stretch and walk, bike or jog briskly

✓ Center after you get home

✓ Practice mindfulness for 3 minutes

One of my clients who found these training techniques particularly helpful is Katy, a professional musician who was living in Europe. She first contacted me toward the end of 2017. Katy had long been working as principal horn with the Philharmonia Orchestra in London. Recently, though, she'd found that she was absolutely hating music. She had too little time to practice, and too much on her schedule. She recalled, "Work had just become just that—work. I was no longer striving for anything beautiful in my sound, there was nothing artistic about it anymore. I was crying before going on stage."

She almost gave up playing the horn, but she knew that there was something inside her that was still there, she just couldn't access it. We needed to work together to help her find her joy in music again and rediscover how it gave purpose and meaning to her life.

First, she needed to learn to focus, just as you have been doing over the past week or so. She started with the centering process, and also began working on her negative self-talk. For so long, whenever she picked up the horn, she would tell herself, "You're going to fuck it up." All her self-hatred about music came through in that moment of picking up the instrument. Centering was difficult for Katy at first, because when it came to seeing, hearing, and feeling what she would do, all she could imagine was how badly it would go. It took a while for Katy to hear herself *not* doing it wrong.

At the time, Katy had an hour-and-a-half train ride into London to go to work and she'd been spending that time simply dreading going to her job. With my help, she started to use that time to center. She would practice centering over and over and over on the train, and one day, she got it! She could see, feel, and hear the performance going right in her mind.

What happened for Katy was that all her practicing of centering paid off. She had slowly been able to turn off the negative mental chatter telling her that as a British person and a woman, she was no good, a failure. She decided to trust the process, even if she didn't yet see the results. Eventually, the process of centering and imagining it going well, became stronger than the negative voice, which slowly faded away.

Unfortunately, by that point, Katy felt so down about music that she left her job with the Philharmonia. Although she was learning to center, she had a lot to overcome in terms of negative feelings about herself. The courage log helped her tremendously. She had been afraid to go into shops, for fear that the shopkeepers would think she wasn't the right sort of customer. She'd been afraid to call people on the phone because she didn't know what they were going to say and couldn't see their faces. She turned down performing jobs because she felt certain she couldn't play them. All this despite the fact she had successfully held a principal position with a major orchestra for several years.

The courage log taught Katy to seek out scary situations. She learned that even if she felt a bubble of fear, that bubble would always be with her, but she could turn the bubble energy to a positive ability to face her fears. Katy explains, "You don't have to live life running away from stuff; you don't have to live in fear. I still do it now. I still will go out and look for things to do that increase my courage. It's those small things that make you realize that you can live every day knowing that you can. And all you need is that foundation of I can. That was truly life changing." It was so life-changing that Katy honestly says she isn't sure what she's afraid of anymore. "I'm quite courageous nowadays. I feel like I'm so courageous that I can't find anything to be really scared of anymore."

After working with me for a year, Katy had gotten very good at centering and mental rehearsal. She found that mental rehearsal helped her not waste time creating bad habits in her playing, going through trial and error to get the good take. "I knew exactly how I was going to play. Exactly how it was going to sound and exactly what it was going to feel like. Only then would I play. For the year after that, whenever I played, I rarely played a mistake because I had already worked that through. My new habit was playing exactly as I wanted to with barely any mistakes, and mistakes didn't really matter anymore because it wasn't about that. It was about how you want this to sound, and that was that."

Even when she was preparing to play in high-pressure situations, like concerts or auditions, situations with real consequences for making mistakes, she knew that if she "vividly imagined my performance going extremely well beforehand, I would create it in reality on stage when the time came. By that time in this work, I firmly believed the ideal performance I had imagined would soon become my real experience, because that's exactly what I mentally practiced and rehearsed over and over in my mind."

On one occasion, though, she had an audition coming up in a week, and despite her preparation and mental rehearsal, she still wanted to push herself to create an experience that was as audition-like as possible. So, she gave a practice audition for a friend—but she did it naked:

> Actually, I decided that fully naked was a bit much, so thought I would do it half-naked. I asked a very, very close friend if I could audition for her naked. In a way it was a bit like how you actually feel in an audition. You feel like they are actually seeing through your soul. You think, oh my God, I wonder what she's thinking about me? Does she think I've got weird boobs? It's the same feeling at an audition. Oh my God, what are they thinking? Are they thinking that they don't like my Beethoven? It was such an amazing experience. I had centered before we started. I got my imagination in line and thought completely through the experience, about what I wanted to focus on and to have my focus and my intentions so strong that I could ignore that I was naked. Knowing that I could see past that gave me so much confidence going into my audition.

What Katy realized, in short, was that after she got her ego out of the way, she was able to stay focused in the here and now on the task at hand. You don't need to perform naked, or even half-naked, but you do need to understand how the ego can get in the way and how you, too, can be focused in the present moment on what you're doing.

The Ego and Being in the Now

What Katy found in her memorable practice audition was that concentration is a temporary state of being where she is totally focused in the continuing present moment of now, such that she could be fully absorbed in what she was doing to the exclusion of everything else, even her own lack of clothing!

What distracts you from this state of mind is the ego, according to Freud's model. The ego likes to be engaged in hyperactive, left-brain thinking, but, as you will see, you can concentrate much better without the over-involvement of your ego. You can think of the ego as the source of the constant stream of thinking that you are unconsciously caught up in. The stream continues when you're awake, offering non-stop analysis, speculation, complaints, labeling, and comparisons. It's the ego that ultimately decides what's unacceptable, undesirable, unwanted, or shouldn't be as it is, or at least in its present form.

The ego likes to be in perpetual motion. It believes that if it is not actively functioning by endless thinking, it will become irrelevant, unnecessary, and perhaps even die. That is why the ego likes to continually wrestle with problems, solve puzzles, hold grudges, and offer its opinions. Many of the ego's near-continuous thoughts are repetitive, and most of them are unnecessary, or even worse, they're judgmental and self-critical.

When the ego encounters problems or challenging situations in the present, it frequently does so with resistance and negativity. The ego resists the current situation because it can't remain in control and alive without thinking continuously about the past or the future, which covers over the reality of the present moment.

To the ego, the present moment in the here and now is relatively boring. The past and the future offer much more to think about—regrets and misgivings about the past, or fears and worries about the future. The past contains one's personal story, and the ego sticks to it as a source of identity, even if it's not helpful to focus on the present moment. From the past, the ego jumps quickly past the present moment and right into the future.

Unfortunately, most of the ego's incessant thoughts are repetitive, negative, and distracting. They keep one from being fully present in the moment, fully aware of what is happening. In addition, most of the ego's thoughts are not in the present moment and are therefore not real. The only thing that is real is the ever continuing and present moment of now. Now is the only time where you have any influence, power, or control.

So how do you get past the ego and its preoccupation with the past and future? Simply and totally by accepting each moment just as it is in the now, without hesitation, resistance, or judgment. You don't have to do anything, other than consciously allow the present moment and current conditions to be the way they already are. Let them continue to be, without your conscious thought or further deliberation. When you do that, you effortlessly enter into the here and now.

You can create a temporary gap in the ego's stream of thoughts by directing the focus of your attention to the continuing present moment. In this way, you draw consciousness away from other mental activity and create a gap of no-mind in which you are highly alert and aware but not thinking. In this focused state, you are fully conscious. In this state, you are much more alert and awake than in the ego-identified state. You are fully present.

The present moment doesn't require much left-brain thought, or any conscious thought at all, which is one reason the ego has a hard time accepting the reality of what is happening in the current present moment. Instead, it thinks and suggests words, it resists and distracts.

Being in the here and now creates a feeling of timelessness by inserting space into the ego's endless stream of thoughts. When your thoughts drift into the past or future, all you need to do is redirect your attention back into the now. Become intensely conscious of the present moment, right here and right now, for as long as you can. Create a gap of thought in the now, not thinking about the past or future. When you do, you will be fully present in the now.

You may be wondering how this is different from what you did in Focus Exercise 2. The previous exercise also asked you to continuously redirect your focus to the present moment, and it asked you to keep aware of thoughts, feelings, sensations, and emotions, as they were occurring in the present. In Focus Exercise 3, you will be working on catching thoughts about the past and future and staying focused on the present moment. It's a subtle difference, and if the two exercises seem similar, that's fine. For now, what you are attempting is to become more aware of how your ego pulls you away from the present moment and into the past or future.

Focus Exercise 3: Being in the Now

"This – the immediate, every day, and present experience, -is IT, the entire ultimate point for the existence of a universe." Alan Watts

1. Sit down
2. Get centered
3. Release any thoughts related to the past or future
4. Focus on the continuing present moment
5. Try to keep your mind present in the now
6. When your attention drifts, redirect it back into the here and now
7. Try to remain there for as long as possible

When you have had your first few glimpses of the moments in between the thoughts of the future or the past, you'll find yourself in a state of timelessness. You'll notice how your mind moves back and forth between the three dimensions of time. You become aware of just how rarely your attention is focused in the now, in comparison to how often your ego has you thinking about the past or future. Just being aware that you are distracted out of the here and now is a mark of success. Knowing that puts you in the present moment, even if it only lasts for a couple of seconds before it is lost again.

As you continue this practice, the moments will last longer and occur more frequently. Practice this exercise now and tomorrow as part of your morning routine. Be sure to take notes about the experience in your journal or notebook.

Judgment versus Discernment

"The practice of discernment is part of higher consciousness. Discernment is not just a step up from judgment. In life's curriculum, it is the opposite of judgment." Glenda Green

When executing complex, coordinated skills in events with real consequences, like competitions, auditions, and recitals, it's easy to judge the performance. However, under pressure, accidents and mistakes happen. In those situations, especially, perfection is impossible. However, many people feel that anything less than perfect might cause a harsh judgment. Judgment can sound like, "that sucks," or, "can't you do any better than that?" You probably can think of more than a few of your own!

The problem with these judgments and negative opinions is that they don't help you correct the problem that you may be experiencing. They only deliver nasty gut punches that make you feel bad, distract you away from the task at hand, and put even more stress on you.

Ignoring accidents or mistakes while you are in the process of executing skills is not the solution. In fact, it can cause even more errors to happen, and possibly injury. After you make a mistake, it's vital that you use discernment rather than judgment. Discernment may sound like, "the note is sharp," or "you're behind the beat." This provides information that can be used to solve the problem, like getting back on the correct pitch or tempo, without the abusive language or unnecessary gut punch.

You certainly don't need any more abusive language or gut-punching. Instead, it's important to develop the habit of being discerning while you are practicing and executing your skills. If you do make a mistake, recognize the error and make the necessary adjustments as soon as possible without unnecessary self-criticism or judgment. That will serve you much better.

Greg spoke about how judgments can cause execution problems, "Especially once you get into high level competition or performance, including a performance for a musical or a one-man show or even a speech in front of a Fortune 500 company. It could be anything, but whatever that performance is, you must be able to not judge it."

Greg had also come to realize that judgment happens in the language-based left brain. "If you're judging in left brain, it takes time to get back to your right brain and the present moment. This is especially true in diving, because there is a three-second window of awareness in a dive. So many divers get stuck because they start analyzing and start judging their own performance while they are still diving. That causes them to miss dives because they are not focused in the moment."

As you practice your skills, take the time to think about and become aware of how judgmental thinking about mistakes is distracting at the very least, and harmful at the worst. Get in the habit of turning your harmful judgments about errors into discernment with implied adjustments. Do not ignore errors or mistakes but correct them in the moment if you are able to, or work on improving them in your future practice sessions.

Creating Successful Events

"That thing always happens that you really believe in; and the belief in a thing makes it happen." Frank Lloyd Wright

Now that you have started to learn techniques to focus and bring you into the present moment, it is time to learn about how to produce peak functioning in real events by using the incredible power of your right-brain imagination and your highly creative mind. This process begins with the way you think about possibilities in upcoming real events. We can start with the idea that thoughts are things. Although we cannot see them or touch them, their effects are real.

As you know, the left brain thinks consciously with words, numbers, logic, calculations, and judgments. The right brain perceives images, physical sensations, sounds, and so on. We all tend to think actively, continuously, and repetitively, except when we are in deep sleep.

Your non-stop thoughts throughout the day can have a strong influence on your behavior, focus, and ultimate outcomes. Thoughts are very creative, and they manifest themselves in the form of physical effects. Your thoughts, especially the repetitive ones that you think over and over, turn into your beliefs, which then form your present reality and shape your future. Thoughts are like magnets that draw real experiences to you, especially in the form of physical effects.

One way to create a successful event, like a championship performance or a winning audition, is through what you imagine to be possible, what you say to yourself and to others, and what you believe you can create to be successful. You need to begin the process with a strong desire for it to ultimately happen one time.

Each event is a single, once-in-a-lifetime occasion. Each one will happen only once in reality. It never really happened before, except in your mind, and it will never happen again the exact same way. It cannot be replicated. Rather than trying to recreate an event, create each event as a new thing, starting in your imagination. Your mental imagery is the first level of creation, with a clear visualization of what you intend to create.

Your words are the second level of creating a desired result. Affirmations help bring your mental pictures and imagery into real form. Words specify your intent and further the creative process that makes an event more likely to occur. Your words and visual projections define your own limits and endless possibilities. Whether you think you can or cannot, you are right. What you think is what you will get in the end.

The process of creating a desired result includes absolute certainty in yourself and your capabilities. You need to believe beyond any doubt whatsoever that you are going to execute your honed skills the way that you intend. In the meantime, you are the one you need to convince about that result. The process includes absolute knowing, at the level of fully assured certainty, that you're absolutely going to execute your refined skills well when the time comes.

In the weeks leading up to the 2008 Legends Reno Tahoe Open, Parker visualized holding the 30-pound trophy over his head. He rehearsed it in front of bathroom mirrors many times. He won at Reno by 7 strokes, including a third round of 62. He received a large, heavy, silver tournament trophy and a check for $540,000. He was on his way to becoming a millionaire. I still have my own photos from the happy event, exactly as he'd visualized it.

Increasing Your Willpower

"The time is always right to do what is right." Martin Luther King, Jr.

Knowing at a high level of certainty involves your sense of personal power. You can further strengthen that power or volition by taking accountabilities for all your thoughts, beliefs, emotions, and actions. Remember William James' theory of willpower? Volition is the process in the mind that directs voluntary movements towards a desired result.

Willing any thought into reality depends upon your knowledge, experience, confidence, willingness, energy, and degree of applied effort. James thought that "if we believe that the end is within our power, we *will* that the desired feeling, having, or doing shall be real, and real it presently becomes, either immediately upon willing or after certain preliminaries have been fulfilled."

This is not necessarily an easy thing to do. You need to shift your thinking from believing that many things are out of your control to believing that you are solely responsible for bringing your intentions and dreams into reality. However, this shift is what you must accomplish to build your willpower and sense of control over your world and your outcomes.

Can you guess what weakens your sense of power to control things? It's fear, causing you to feel helpless, blaming unfortunate circumstances, or claiming that most things are out of your control. Any of these habits can put you into a victim mentality that will diminish your power. You may excuse your shortcomings by citing a lack of proper training, bad teachers, inadequate conditions, or poor equipment, but this will diminish your willpower and sense of total control.

One caveat is needed, of course: Certain things are obviously outside your immediate sphere of influence. You cannot really change others or affect their behavior in any significant way without their consent. Nor can you violate the laws of science, like gravity, and affect what is out of your physical control. However, whatever your current circumstance may be, you can control your attitude and your response to it.

You first need to accept that there are certain things that are beyond your influence. Remember how you practiced accepting reality just as it comes to you in our second focus exercise? Choose to make the best of each situation, at least for the time being. All conditions are temporary and subject to change. Focus on doing your best regardless of external circumstances or anyone else. Realize that your power does not come from outside of yourself, but from within. It is fueled by a strong desire for excellence and supported by high confidence and courage.

You can build your willpower by deciding that from now on you are going to take full responsibility on a daily and continuing basis for everything over which you do have control. Focus on the activities, projects, tasks, thoughts, and behaviors that will lead to your success. These include your physical and mental practice habits, your morning routine, and doing the recommended exercises. Make sure that you are ready to accept total responsibility for everything that happens that you can control everyday—and forget everything else. That is easier said than done, but it's essential.

Once you become accountable and responsible for everything under your control, you stop looking for excuses or someone to blame for mistakes. When you're willing to acknowledge your principal role in mishaps, you will see their real cause clearly and you will be able to imagine different solutions to those problems. This starts the process of actively turning your intentions and desires into reality.

The Power of Imagination

"Nothing happens unless first a dream." Carl Sandburg.

Let's go back to Parker, the former PGA golf player. After his success, he was trying to figure out how to move forward with his life now that it was no longer about shooting low scores and winning tournaments. His wife and new family needed him in more ways than just being a loving husband and father.

Parker explored several new opportunities instead of trying to get back on tour. He commentated for a while on the Golf Channel and the PGA Tour Live Show but broadcasting on TV wasn't a good fit for him. He served as an assistant coach with the UCLA golf team for a while, but that didn't quite feel right either. Then he started working with PGA Tour players on their short game and soon found that he was getting some excellent results. Parker was a great right-brain player with a super touch around the greens, and he possessed an awesome imagination. He just needed to put all that to good use in a new endeavor.

In golf, the short game involves any shots that are within a hundred yards of the hole, such as chip shots, pitches, and bunker shots from the sand traps. Parker had always been very good at those shots and able to help other players with their own short game shots. He started looking into how to help even high-level players, so they could have better short games. "That came down to the question of how can they set up properly to hit all the different shots with their wedges around the green correctly? Once I discovered how to do that, how to set them up properly to do a chip shot, pitch, or a bunker shot, they tended to hit great shots."

Parker felt like he was 85% of the way to really helping these golfers score better by hitting those shots more effectively. But he wanted to be able to help golfers without being there in person. He wondered, "Is there something I could put on a golf club that would give a visual reference for the correct positioning of their hands on the club? It would clearly show them how to place their hands at the right angle to hit an effective shot."

That's when he came up with the idea for alignment-enhanced lines on wedges (wedges are the clubs players use around the greens). The lines on the club would set the proper angle for the intended shot. The lines would help show where to put your hands, whether it was a high or low shot, or from the short grass or long stuff, or from the sand in the bunker. That was sort of the genesis behind that new idea. Parker's imaginative playing led him to a breakthrough new idea in his beloved game of golf, and it can have transformative effects on your skills, too.

Here are the things that I would recommend that you do today or during this step:

- Practice intermediate centering at least 4 times
- Continue with your courage log with 3 brave acts
- Practice the focus exercise of being in the now 3 times
- Write down how you will change your judgements into discernment
- List the ways you can use to create desired events in reality
- Imagine everything going well
- Write down the things you are doing to build your willpower
- Strive for excellence
- Plan on following your routine in the morning

Week 2

Thursday or Step 9

"There is only one corner of the universe you can be certain are improving, and that's your own self. "Aldous Huxley

Now, you will learn even more about concentration, as you continue practicing it and completing your morning routine. We will be covering beta, alpha, and gamma waves as measured on an electroencephalogram (EEG), one-pointed concentration, and the first four levels of Abraham Maslow's Hierarchy of Needs.

Morning Routine:

- ✓ Wake up to energizing music
- ✓ Drink 8 oz water
- ✓ Splash cold water on your face at least 7 times
- ✓ Get outside within minutes
- ✓ Stretch and walk, bike or jog briskly
- ✓ Center after you get home
- ✓ Practice mindfulness for 3 minutes

Let me introduce you to a very talented musician who was struggling with her upcoming graduate recitals. Although she grew up in Greece, Athina was completing her master's degree in music at the Sibelius Academy in Helsinki. She knew that she would need to start preparing for her graduate exams, which included a series of recitals in front of faculty members and other students.

Athina had experienced some difficulties with her performances at the Academy before she left, and her assessments helped us both to understand why. We learned that she was only able to perform well if she was relaxed. When her energy spiked, which it usually did before and during important performances, she could not control it. Athina's confidence was also at an all-time low due to her critical self-talk, pessimistic attitude, and inability to imagine performing her best. She had low scores in courage, with many fears and strong doubts that clearly showed up in her playing.

Fortunately, like many musicians, Athina had high scores for motivation, commitment, and mental toughness. That would help. I began teaching her centering to control and channel her nervous energy and becoming more optimistic, with positive self-talk and affirmations. After several sessions, she was making definite progress with certain skills, like mental rehearsal, but hadn't progressed very much in other critical areas.

We started to reflect on what might be getting in her way, and she reported that she felt like there was "something inside of me preventing me from experiencing my best. I was coming up with different negative emotions. One emotion was bringing up something that led to another, and then we would work through that one."

We started with fear, which is at the bottom on the emotional scale. Athina's feelings of fear had a major influence on her ability to perform well, especially in moments when it really mattered. It also affected her daily life, and not in a good way. Understanding her fears, completing her courage history, and performing 21 acts of courage certainly made her a more courageous person and performer, but we still needed to address her other negative emotions.

The next emotions that we worked through were anxiety, anger, discouragement, and blame. One by one, we progressed through these negative emotions, and then we moved on to forgiveness. As she said, "Forgiveness was related to understanding myself, and also to others and my particular surroundings. It involved bad memories that were related to people that took place in my life. I was still carrying most of those with me and they were coming up in random moments, preventing me from paying attention to the music and causing me to mess up in many of my performances." Athina needed to learn and practice the vital act of forgiveness if she was ever going to succeed.

Regardless of what Athina experienced in her past, she needed to let it go. If she was ever going to achieve peak functioning, she needed to learn how to practice the art of forgiveness.

Brainwaves

Over the past several days, we have talked a lot about how the brain works, including the left and right brains and different psychological ideas about how the different parts of our selves affect our functioning. We've talked about the power of thoughts to create desired realities, and we've spent time working on different ways to focus your attention.

Now we're going to turn to a very scientific way of looking at the brain, which will help you further understand what goes into creating desired events and peak functioning. You may have heard of the device that measures the electrical activity in the brain. It is called an electroencephalogram, or EEG for short. For the EEG, several small, flat metal discs are attached to specific points on the scalp that are then wired to a computer, which displays the electrical brain wave patterns on an oscilloscope. These wave patterns can be measured by how many wavelengths appear on the screen per second (known as cycles per second, or cps).

Brain Waves

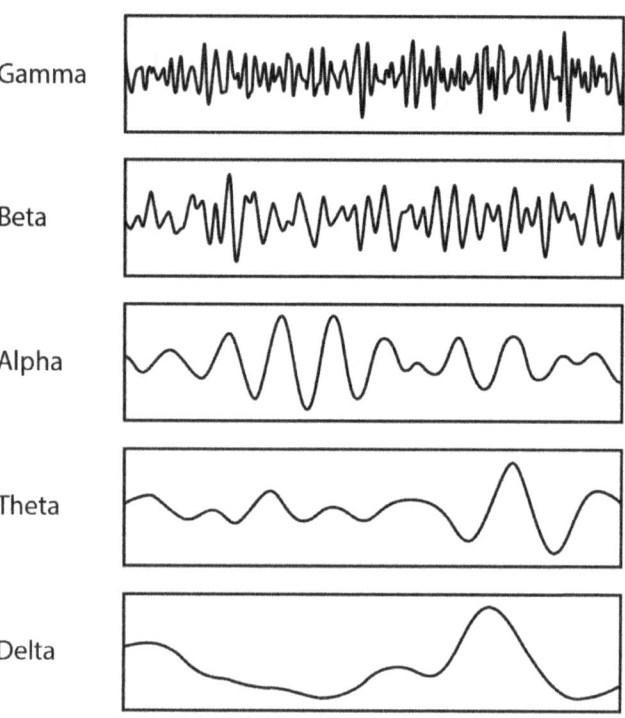

The left hemisphere of the brain tends to race at high speed, with a type of mental processing known as beta waves. Beta brain waves measure from 13–37 cycles per second (cps), which is very fast. On an oscilloscope, beta looks like a high-amplitude, choppy pattern with a series of spikes that happen really fast. Focus cannot occur when the left hemisphere is too active.

Beta thoughts are scattered and highly distracting. They jump back and forth between past mistakes and future worries. They often involve thinking about places other than where you are and doing something other than what you are currently doing. The left brain's high activity consists of unending analyses, worries, judgments, criticisms, blaming, doubting, rationalizing, planning, commenting, giving instructions, and offering personal opinions.

These all cause the mind to race at even higher speeds. The faster it goes, the more you will be distracted away from the task at hand in the moment. Beta may be the normal state of waking consciousness in a fast-paced and left-brained world, but this type of thinking is not at all helpful for performers and athletes who need a focused mindset when under pressure. Concentration cannot happen when the left hemisphere is highly active and racing at beta's breakneck speeds. Before you perform or compete, you need to get out of your noisy and distracting left brain and its beta thinking.

In order to concentrate, including while doing the next focusing exercise, you need to get out of your noisy left brain and into your quiet right brain, focused in the alpha state. Alpha waves are much slower than beta waves and range from 4 cps to 7 cps. On an oscilloscope, alpha looks smoother than the sharp-angled, high-frequency beta waves. The flowing alpha waves reflect a relaxed, but highly focused, right-brain state. Alpha is much better than beta for focusing on executing a series of complex, coordinated movements in the present moment.

Alpha sets up a concentrated right-brain flow state uninterrupted by left-brain thoughts, analyses, judgments, comparisons, doubts, instructions, criticisms, worries, or fears. You must be able to shift on command to the focused, right-brain state of alpha before you execute your skills. The centering process is specifically designed to get you into the focused alpha state in a relatively short time, wherever you are. After centering, you can consciously enter alpha through unconditional acceptance and non-resistance of what is happening in the here and now.

One-pointed Concentration

"One great cause of failure is lack of concentration." Bruce Lee

The fastest brain waves most people experience are left-brain beta waves. Beta brain waves of low frequencies (13–20 cps) are indicative of uneasiness or mild anxiety. Mid-frequency beta waves (21–30 cps) appear during extreme anxiety. The highest beta frequencies (31–37 cps) are manifest in panic attacks and the inability to focus or function effectively.

However, there is an even higher brain wave frequency than beta. It is known as gamma, and it can be extremely beneficial in the execution of complex skills. Gamma waves are the fastest in the human spectrum, measuring from 38–100 cps. Gamma is the frequency experienced when in a state of flow, peak functioning, or being in "the zone" and peak functioning. (If you don't know what all of these mean, don't worry, we will learn about them soon.)

Gamma waves originate in the thalamus, a concentrated mass of gray matter in the midbrain region. The waves move quickly to the amygdala, suppressing any fight/flight responses, then to the entire prefrontal cortex, and then back again to the base brain. This all happens 30 times per second, or even faster. This full-sweep action throughout the brain creates a state of neural synchrony associated with peak functioning.

Gamma patterns in the brain regulate emotional levels. They heighten sensory awareness and the ability to achieve total concentration. Gamma is associated with feeling calm, happy, joyful, and grateful, "blissed out" beyond the ego, experiencing unity and universal love. This euphoric state is well known by mystics, such as Christian monks, Zen masters, and Indian yogis. It is also found in individuals when they are in flow, fully engaged in challenging activities that require their highest level of concentration.

These masters are able to remain in the here and now of the continuing and ever-changing present moment, with a laser-like focus on the one challenging task in which they're fully engaged, wrapped up in a cocoon of concentration. They become totally absorbed in what they are doing in the here and now, immersed in the activity or task to the exclusion of everything else in the world. The sense of separateness between their egos or identities and the activity in which they are engaged disappears.

During more ordinary thinking states, the ego makes a clear distinction between oneself and everything and everyone else in the world, including any activities you are presently engaged in. Your ego will continually try to convince you that you are a separate entity, unconnected to anything or anyone outside of yourself. When you are able to get past the sense of separateness created by your ego, you will reach the state of oneness between subject and object, or between you and the activity or event you're engaged in.

This merging of two into one is necessary to attain a state of intensely focused attention or one-pointed concentration in gamma. In the Japanese martial art of Zen archery, the master and the target become one. In this state of oneness, there are no thoughts of individual separation being created by the ego, because the gamma wave state has temporarily silenced the ego's noisy chatter and has brought you into the present moment of now.

The next exercise is designed to help you reach the gamma state of mind through the practice of one-pointed concentration.

Focus Exercise 4: One-Pointed Concentration

1. Put a candle on a table in front of you, below your eye level.
2. Set a timer for two minutes.
3. Light the candle.
4. Get centered, preferably using the candle as your focal point.
5. Look at the flame. Keep your eyes fixed there.
6. Do nothing but focus totally only on the flame with your narrowed gaze.
7. If you have any thoughts other than your connection with the flame, disregard them.
8. Focus back on the flame.
9. Do this for two minutes or as long as possible.

Practice one-pointed concentration today and as you practice it, you will notice an increase in your ability to focus intensely on one thing in the present moment. Make notes about the experience in your journal or notebook. We will return to the focusing exercises during the week before the final live performance event.

The fifth component of peak functioning is focusing exclusively on the task at hand in the here and now.

The Hierarchy of Needs

"In any given moment we have two options: to step forward into growth or to step back into safety." Abraham Maslow

Dr. Abraham Maslow, the American psychologist who developed the motivational model known as the "hierarchy of needs" and the concept of self-actualization, can help you understand why this possible difficulty makes perfect sense. He founded the human potential movement in psychology. Maslow studied highly functioning individuals in a variety of fields to understand how they developed their amazing capabilities, realized their highest potentials, and achieved incredible success.

Maslow's research included exceptional individuals throughout history like Ludwig van Beethoven, Thomas Jefferson, Henry David Thoreau, and Abraham Lincoln. He also closely observed the behavior of outstanding people of his time, including Albert Einstein, Nobel laureate Jane Addams, Gestalt psychologist Max Wertheimer, First Lady Eleanor Roosevelt, the healthiest 1% of college graduates in the United States, and many elite performing artists and champion athletes.

Maslow wanted to understand what motivated these people to realize their highest potential and achieve unprecedented success in their lives and careers. He discovered that all people, including highly functioning individuals, are motivated according to their current specific level of needs, and that these needs can be arranged in a hierarchical, pyramid-like structure of distinct steps or levels.

Hierarchy of Needs

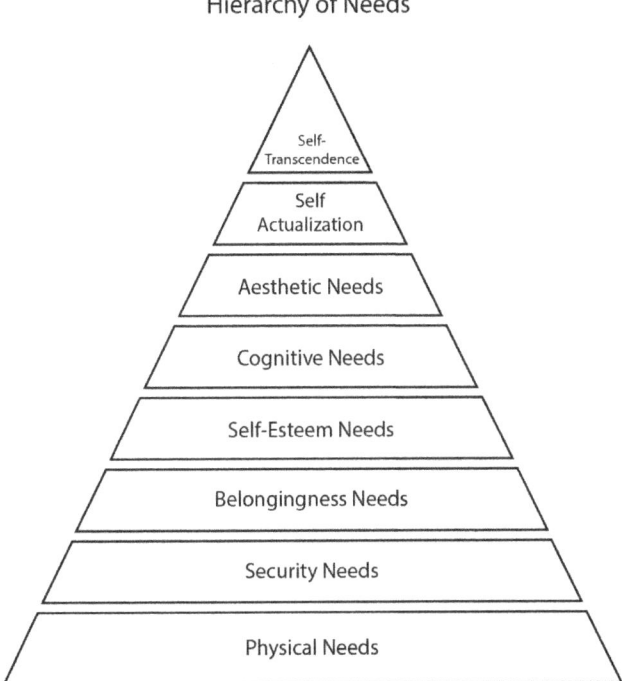

The updated version of Maslow's original hierarchy includes eight different levels of needs. The first stage or level, at the base of the pyramid, includes the most basic human needs. These physical, biological, or survival needs include air, water, food, warmth, clothing, rest, and sleep. Unless those basic needs are satisfied, people are not motivated to move up to the next level. After the needs of this level are met, however, individuals are then motivated to move up the ladder.

The second level includes needs related to security or safety, such as needing to feel personally protected from danger in the environment or from harm by others. It also includes the need of a safe and stable place to live, with freedom from fear and the financial resources to secure that place to live. At a most basic level, people in our contemporary world need money and several other resources to satisfy their needs on the first two levels.

Once those basic needs for physical survival and security are met, people are motivated to have their social needs met. These needs are found on the third level. They're described as "belongingness needs," or the need to be accepted as part of a social community and have a sense of connection with others in that group. You may not usually think of your social affiliations and interpersonal contacts with family, friends, co-workers, clubs, schools, and teams as needs, but they are. We need intimate relationships with significant others, as well as love, emotional support, kindness, trust and affection. After we have them, though, we tend to become interested in the next level, which involves being a respected member of our communities.

The fourth stage in Maslow's hierarchy is the need for self-esteem or self-respect. There are two types involved in this level of need. The first is the value that one has for oneself, with a corresponding sense of power, strength, control, achievement, competence, pride, dignity, autonomy, independence, integrity, and mastery. The other aspect of this level is the desire for respect from others in your world and involves your perceived reputation, status, and prestige.

These first four levels in the hierarchy are known as *deficit needs*. These needs only motivate people when they are not satisfied or fulfilled. Once they are fulfilled, there is no reason to change your behavior to acquire them. After a big meal at home with family and friends to celebrate your most recent victory, you likely don't feel like you need more food, a different home, or desire for the company of other people.

Until you're hungry again, or you find yourself needing a different type of home or place to stay, or you're on the outs with your friends or family, not feeling good about yourself or your reputation in your community. Then you'd likely try to achieve what's missing, to have your basic needs met. You'd look for a new home, get a job to pay for it, make amends with your friends or family, or change your behavior to be held in better esteem.

Unfortunately, many people get caught up in a revolving cycle, fluctuating endlessly between the first four levels, due mainly to the reality of how hard it can be to satisfy those needs. They get stuck trying to take care of the real demands associated with those levels, without meeting them on a continuing or permanent basis. Whether those deficit needs are for survival, security, social relationship, or self-esteem, if they are not met, they will prevent the person from reaching the higher levels of the pyramid.

In order to achieve peak functioning, though, you'll need to move out of the deficit levels and into the levels that meet other needs. We'll talk about those next. For now, here are the things that I would recommend that you do today or during this step:

- Practice Intermediate centering at least 5 times
- Continue with your courage log with 3 brave acts
- Practice the Focus Exercise 4 of one-pointed concentration 3 times
- Stick with your morning routine to continue building your personal power
- Write down the other things you are doing to build your volition
- Laugh out loud for at least a few minutes
- Write out five things you can do to strive for excellence
- Plan on following your routine in the morning

Friday or Step 10

*Y*our second live performance event is coming up. It should go much better than the last time, if you have been keeping up with everything that we've been doing. Today, you will learn about the upper four levels of the hierarchy of needs, peak experiences, self-actualization, the zone, flow states, and the tapering process. All of these will help you have a much-improved performance.

Morning Routine:

- ✓ Wake up to energizing music
- ✓ Drink 8 oz water
- ✓ Splash cold water on your face at least 7 times
- ✓ Get outside within minutes
- ✓ Stretch and walk, bike or jog briskly
- ✓ Center after you get home
- ✓ Practice mindfulness for 3 minutes

"Find the good. It's all around you. Find it, showcase it, and you'll start believing it." Jesse Owens

To continue our ascendence through the Hierarchy of Needs, I'd like to introduce you to a truly incredible man, Dylan Skye Hart. In a way, his struggle to improve his career relates to the hierarchy of needs. Although he had achieved a high level of success as a gig musician and was financially stable, he contacted me because he wanted to land an audition for a contracted position with a top-level orchestra. He'd taken care of the first three levels, but he felt a need to improve his self-esteem by landing a job with a top-tier symphony, something his skills qualified him to do.

I first met Dylan in 2014. At the time, he was a very successful Los Angeles-based recording musician working in the major studios in Hollywood. He went on to play principal horn on nearly one-hundred movies, including *Jumanji: The Next Level*, *Jungle Cruise*, and *Star Wars: The Rise of Skywalker*. However, despite his amazing talent and great practice habits, he kept hitting the wall with professional auditions. In just the past few years, he had taken more than thirty auditions, but he had never landed the big job.

Recently, Dylan had been getting to the semi-finals, finals, and even the super-finals in auditions, but it seemed like he just couldn't win. He eventually realized that he was self-sabotaging, but at the time, he was only superficially aware of what was holding him back. He did not realize the debilitating effect this was having on his execution.

Looking back, Dylan realized:

> Every time I would go out for a major orchestral audition, I would think about the repercussions of what would happen if I actually won, like having to move away from my hometown, my family, and everything. I was afraid of the changes that could come with winning something big, because I wasn't going out for something small. I was already making enough money as a recording artist. In order for me to make it worthwhile to move, the job would have to be with the New York Phil, LA Phil, or

something on that level, so it was really hard for me to deal with the fear of success. If you attain success, then you won't have time to indulge in the other activities that you really like.

In order to succeed, though, he needed to learn how to get out of his own way. At the time, he was preparing for an audition with the Los Angeles Philharmonic. As usual, we started with a battery of assessments, which helped clarify his complexity. His learning profile showed that he was a very good learner but had a low frustration tolerance. Dylan's assessment on peak performance indicated that he was willing to play the edge, but he did not have a consistent routine before he played. His competitive styles assessment depicted high confidence, positive and affirming self-talk, and little if any fear of failure. Unfortunately, he had low focus scores and a surprisingly strong fear of success.

One of the first things that Dylan did was to complete his extensive courage history, both in music and his normal life. We soon realized that he was a very courageous individual in general, but he had struggled with his success in music in the past. However, it had never really stopped him until now. He thought that he was ready to take the quantum leap past his fear of success in order to win a major audition.

Before that happened, Dylan and I needed to resolve important aspects of his audition execution that he had not yet figured out, including getting past his fear of success. Just like you have done, we started with basic centering, his courage history and courage log, practicing mental rehearsal, making important changes based on discernment rather than judgment, following a pre-performance routine, and strengthening his willpower. I soon realized that Dylan already knew a lot about focus, flow states, and peak functioning, which was how he had already become one of the most successful horn players in the LA studios. Nevertheless, Dylan felt driven to grow further and achieve on an even higher level.

Growth Needs

"I'm in constant pursuit of growing and evolving." Alicia Key

The top four levels of the hierarchy of needs are known as *growth needs*. These needs arise not from a lack of something (like food, shelter, etc.), but from a desire to grow or expand as a human being. As opposed to deficit needs, which bring decreased motivation when they are met, motivation for growth needs *increases* when they are satisfied. The individual wants more of the same and is motivated to do what it takes to attain that feeling again, causing more growth.

The fifth level in the hierarchy represents the cognitive or intellectual needs. These involve the thirst for knowledge, the desire for deeper understanding, and the continual search for meaning and wisdom. It's the human need to learn, explore, discover, and reach a better understanding of the world around us as well as of ourselves. It requires never-ending curiosity and wonder, and it also involves a complimentary need for reason, predictability, and personal meaning.

The sixth level involves aesthetic needs and the appreciation of beauty in a colorful kaleidoscope of diverse expressions. Beauty is what we find pleasing, especially to the visual and auditory senses. It is a combination of attractive qualities, like shape, color, form, order, sound, grace, symmetry, and harmony. Beauty touches our artistic senses through music, dance, poetry, art, and nature, bringing joy, appreciation, meaning, and a healthy desire for more.

Self-actualization and Peak Experiences

"If you do follow your bliss you put yourself on a kind of track that has been there all the while, waiting for you, and the life that you ought to be living is the one you are living... Follow your bliss and don't be afraid, and doors will open where you didn't know they were going to be." Joseph Campbell

The next level of Maslow's hierarchy is self-actualization, which he originally included as part of the top of the pyramid, but which now occupies one rung from the top. Even so, it is thought that only a few people reach this level. At this level, one experiences the need to realize and express one's full potential, capabilities, and unique talents. Self-actualization is driven by the powerful desire to become everything that one is capable of actually becoming. It means achieving and demonstrating the greatest version of the grandest vision of who you really are. It includes a strong desire for personal growth, rather than deficit-driven motivational force like the lower-level needs.

Maslow identified common characteristics or qualities shared by self-actualized individuals: feeling integrated, whole, and complete, with the ability to tolerate the uncertainty of opposites; being spontaneous in thought and action; task-centered vs. self-centered; highly creative, playful, happy, autonomous, resourceful, independent, and comfortable being alone; totally accepting of things, others, and oneself just the way they are, with sincere gratitude.

The final level of the pyramid is called self-transcendence, and it is here that we find what are called "peak experiences." The final level involves spiritual needs or the desire for self-transcendence. It is related to the human quest for altered states of consciousness and refers to the need to reach another state of mind or a subjective experience that is beyond one's normal state of conscious awareness.

Peak experiences are highly valued, transient moments, lasting from seconds to minutes, when individuals experience their highest levels of integration, harmony, and functioning. These exciting and uplifting experiences are the primary desire for those who have attained this highest level. They often reported that their intense experiences were accompanied by heightened states of awareness, ecstasy, aliveness, euphoria, and insight, with a broadened perspective.

Maslow considered peak experiences to be mystical states, involving feelings of profound wonder, meaning, and joy. While having them, people felt in total control of their body, mind, emotions, as well as some of the external conditions in their environment. They also perceived a change in their relative time and space orientation, with time slowing down or stopping briefly, and feeling a powerful energy that was suddenly at their disposal to use however they wanted.

Maslow found that there were several common attributes or qualities that helped individuals achieve their highest level of superior functioning. These were engaging fully with live, with openness, courage, wonder, awe, gratitude, as well as being happy, having fun, being spontaneous in moment, honesty with oneself and others, taking full responsibility and accountability for their actions, working diligently, especially on oneself, and dealing with problems should they arise, without creating them.

Self-actualized or fully realized individuals have a willingness to risk being vulnerable, even to look silly, and they examine the painful parts of their personalities to learn and grow. They have a healthy, non-hostile sense of humor and the ability to laugh at themselves. Maslow thought that no one was perfect, especially self-actualizers. They simply had developed the ability to accept themselves fully, with all their faults, without judgment

Flow States

"Be still like a mountain and flow like a great river." Lao Tzu

Finally, we must add one other piece to the puzzle of achieving peak performances, and that is experiences of being in flow. This experience was first described in 1993 by Dr. Mihaly Csikszentmihalyi (pronounced me-high cheek-send-me-high-ee), a professor at the University of Chicago who was originally from Croatia.

Dr. C. interviewed more than 8,000 individuals about the quality of their life experiences when they were totally engaged in enjoyable yet challenging activities. These experiences included competitive sports, music, dance, skiing, martial arts, rock climbing, interactive games, and creative projects. The individuals all described a similar experience that he called being in "flow."

The flow state has five major characteristics: clarity, commitment, centering, continuing feedback, and challenge. Clarity of intention means setting clear goals, knowing what you intend to accomplish, and planning how you're going to do it. You've already known your overarching goal: to reach a peak level of functioning in your upcoming performance, by following your training regimen and performance routines. You also have experience in setting a smaller goal when you set your clear intention during the centering process.

The ability to commit yourself totally to achieving your intention involves the firm decision to trust your whole self to move past your ego and beyond your fears. If you hold back and play it safe, you will never get in flow or reach your highest level of functioning. You need to decide ahead of time that you will go for it and let it fly, holding nothing back when the moment comes, no matter what.

Centering means being in the right-brain state of alpha, quietly focused in the here and now on the task at hand. The centering process is specifically designed to shift you into that ideal performance mindset before you begin. You can also use centering to quickly get to alpha back if you lose flow during your performance. Next, getting continuing feedback means that you must receive immediate, correct, and continuing information about how you are doing in the here and now. You need to be fully aware in the present moment whether you are on track and executing your skills correctly.

The fifth characteristic of getting in flow is having the right balance between the difficulty of the challenge and the perceived ability to meet that challenge. The task's level of difficulty needs to match the confidence necessary to be in flow. When the task is too easy, it does not require full involvement or total attention. Before long, people get bored and become easily distracted. If the demand of the task is far beyond their perceived level of confidence to accomplish, they will start to feel intimidated, anxious, and frustrated, and they are at risk of giving up.

When a highly challenging situation demands your best, you reach a state of total focus, where less critical concerns and distractions fade away or disappear. People in flow move beyond the mindset of everyday consciousness, with life's daily frustrations, worries, and doubts. Someone who is in a state of flow isn't worrying about their unpaid bills; a rock climber isn't thinking about a problem back at the office. Not only can they not afford to let their minds wander—that would result in a missed note for the musician, or a disastrous fall for the climber—but flow also involves a single-minded absorption and total concentration in the moment when involved in a very challenging event or activity.

In the flow state, the focus of attention that is usually split between two or more things merges into a single, highly concentrated "laser beam" of directed attention. People who are in flow are much more focused and efficient in their actions. They tend to produce extraordinary results with effortless power, rather than putting forth powerless effort.

The normal sense of time is distorted when one is in a state of flow. Hours can seem to pass in a few minutes, and one can experience a sense of timelessness. Other times, like when a ballet dancer is spinning on her toes, moments seem to stretch out and out and out, taking an unusually long time. The subjective perception of time changes when you're in flow, or even when observing someone else who is engaged in flow, and it also changes when you're in what is called "the zone."

The Zone

"I mean, we all fly. Once you leave the ground, you fly. Some people fly longer than others." Michael Jordan

Several years ago, sport science researchers asked elite athletes about their highest levels of performance. Many of the athletes described feeling like they were in a zone of exceptional execution and superior functioning. Their experiences had several common characteristics: they described an absence of fear, being intensely focused, a sense of full absorption in the activity, and feeling godlike, in total control of themselves and their immediate surroundings. They perceived everything as being integrated, unified, and whole, and they often experienced a sense of timelessness. In other words, they were describing being in flow, even if they didn't use that language.

Researchers also explored the conditions that produced peak functioning in sports. These conditions included the athletes being intensely engaged in the activity or skill while being physically relaxed. The athletes reported high levels of confidence, being focused exclusively on accomplishing the task at hand, and adapting quickly and effectively to the ever-changing demands of reality.

The experience of a peak performance and being in the zone for most athletes was preceded by an optimistic expectation of anticipated success. Success felt not only possible but highly probable. They trusted their talent, training, and experience unconditionally, which let them go for it and let it fly, holding absolutely nothing back. The athletes reported that they were intensely focused on what they were doing in the moment and felt like they were in a cocoon of concentration.

The athletes who experienced peak functioning and being in the zone felt like they possessed exceptional power and control over their skills and the situation. This was a performance level way beyond the ordinary. After the peak performance, the athletes often experienced an elevated level of self-validation and fulfillment accompanied by feelings of wonder, joy, and gratitude, as well as a sense of transcendence.

Performing in flow in the zone is the sixth component of peak functioning.

As you are no doubt beginning to understand, the exercises you have been working on are all geared towards helping you achieve a state of flow and being in the zone. Neuroscience confirms these states when your brain experiences gamma waves. As the athletes who described being in the zone realized, their intense training also played into the event as they were able to fully imagine and create their ideal positive experiences. All of this will be essential for helping you achieve peak functioning in your upcoming event.

Dylan, the French horn player, already knew about playing in flow and being in the zone when we met. Here's what he said about this experience:

> It's about being incredibly aware in the present moment, because if you are thinking about the past, then you're not focused on what you're doing, and the past doesn't even exist because it's already happened. If you're thinking about the future, then you're not focused on what you're doing, and the future doesn't exist, either, because that hasn't happened yet. Just being present, just enjoying what you're doing in the moment that you're doing it makes everything slow down.

> I think that slowing down is a by-product of being present, because when you're thinking about the past or future in clock time, then you're essentially speeding up your internal clock because you're not noticing the seconds that tick by. You have to focus on being in the moment and not focus past it. Peak functioning occurs when you are flawlessly executing your plan and everything just kind of happens. It's being in that state of flow and not getting in your way, just allowing your body to do all of the things that it knows how to do. Everything just kind of happens.

> Flawless execution is an interesting thing, because there is such a thing, but it comes in small spurts, right? But none of it is about being perfect. It's about being present and following through with your intentions. With all this preparation, you set yourself up to achieve your intentions without getting in your own way, which can provide you with essentially flawless execution. By "flawless," I don't mean that there aren't any mistakes whatsoever. I do not know any professionals who never make a mistake.

I think that being in the zone and in the flow state is about as good as you can get as far as flawless execution goes, because then at least you're doing everything that you possibly can do to execute your plan to achieve your highest level of functioning. It's not about trying to prevent mistakes. It's about not allowing those mistakes to change your focus.

Here are the things that I would recommend that you do today or during this step:

- Practice intermediate centering at least 6 times
- Continue your courage log with 3 brave acts
- Commit to at least 3 courageous actions during your upcoming performance
- Practice one-pointed concentration 3 times
- List the things you need to do to be in flow in the zone
- Imagine everything going well
- Write down the things you are doing to build your willpower
- Strive for excellence
- Plan on following your routine in the morning

Saturday

*W*elcome to your second live performance event. Once again, you can start whenever you are ready, but you only get one chance to execute your skills at the highest level possible. Before then, use your mind, positive thoughts, affirmations and willpower to create a successful event in reality. Imagine your ideal execution vividly from beginning to end. Summon up all your courage, as you commit to playing the edge. Strive for excellence.

Morning Routine:

✓ Wake up to energizing music

✓ Drink 8 oz water

✓ Splash cold water on your face at least 7 times

✓ Get outside within minutes

✓ Stretch and walk, bike or jog briskly

✓ Center after you get home

✓ Practice mindfulness for 3 minutes

Try to get beyond your ego. Focus your mind exclusively on the task at hand in the here and now. Get ready to be in the zone in flow and have some fun. Get yourself centered in right brain in alpha or gamma in one-pointed concentration. Then smile before you go for it and let it fly! Once you start, do not stop until you reach the end.

Afterwards, take a break before you review the event and your performance. Then, in your journal or notebook, evaluate your performance honestly and objectively. Give yourself a rating or score from 1–99 (poor to peak) in each of the categories:

Centered _____

Positive mindset _____

Confidence _____

Courage _____

Focus _____

In flow in the zone _____

Execution _____

In your journal or notebook, note all the things that you did extremely well, especially if you had any moments of being in flow in the zone and peak functioning. Capture those in writing. What was your experience? What did these look like? How did they sound? How did they feel? You need to vividly and repeatedly imagine those things in complete detail as they happened in reality. It's worth the time to do it right now, while the memory of your execution is fresh and accurate.

Then consider the things that still need improvement. List those in your journal or notebook and then once again, prioritize them. Put them on your agenda to work on next week. Consider how you can work on them during your morning routine.

"Don't let the same dog bite you twice." Chuck Berry

In the meantime, take care of any errands that may need your attention before next week, and then try to relax for the rest of the day. Take it easy. Treat yourself to the rewards and symbols that you deserve for your efforts thus far in your journey. Next week may prove to be very challenging for you, but there is nothing you cannot handle, especially with your ever-increasing courage, focus and willpower.

Monday or Step 11

Now we will be venturing into different territory. We'll take a close look at Jungian psychology, and specifically, Jung's ideas about the personal and collective unconscious, archetypes, the persona, and the shadow. We will start by examining your focus during last Saturday's performance, including any unforced errors and what may have caused you to be distracted. Lack of focus is a major cause of execution mistakes. As I hope you are starting to realize, it's important that you take full responsibility for what keeps you from doing your best.

Morning Routine:

- ✓ Wake up to energizing music
- ✓ Drink 8 oz water
- ✓ Splash cold water on your face at least 7 times
- ✓ Get outside within minutes
- ✓ Stretch and walk, bike or jog briskly
- ✓ Center after you get home
- ✓ Practice mindfulness for 3 minutes

Review your journal or notebook entries from after the event and consider the most serious errors that you made during the performance. What kept you from being focused right before the mistakes happened? Was it your left-brain thoughts, judgments, or outcome thoughts? Did you allow your mind to drift, wander, or zone out when you were executing? Were you thinking back to a previous mistake, or anticipating a potential problem that might happen? What caused you to lose your focus? Make notes about these important things.

Now you are ready to learn the advanced form of centering. Advanced centering can be done anywhere, anytime, sitting, standing, or even moving, in less than 10 seconds. Start by finding a comfortable and balanced position, either sitting or standing. Your feet should feel solid on the floor, with your back straight, your hands over your center. Choose your clear intention and say it to yourself. Pick your focal point and then soften your gaze to a general area on the floor in front of you. You will remember these steps from your previous experiences with centering.

On the first inhale, breathe slowly and mindfully into your center. Pause, and as you exhale the first breath, drop all the tension you feel in your upper body. During the second breath, be at your center. Get out of your head and into your center. During the third breath, vividly imagine your performance going just the way you intend. Then let the energy come up from your center up to your eyes, open them, and then look at your focal point. You are now centered and ready to perform your best.

Advanced Centering

1. Breathe into your center and drop tension

2. Be at your center

3. Imagine it the way you intend

That is the advanced form of the centering process. As always, I recommend that you practice this form twice today and then more times every day for the next several days. Keep track of your practice sessions in your journal or notebook. Here is what Dylan had to say about centering:

> For me, centering is a really, really effective and fast way to get into that place where you can be in a state of flow. Centering brings all of your energy into one spot of your body, and then you allow that energy to be focused into the now.
>
> Basic and intermediate centering are the building blocks for getting to advanced centering. Basic centering takes a while to do. You have to sit down and relax, check in on all your muscles and make sure that you're not holding tension anywhere. The intermediate form is that same thing, but slightly shortened. Then advanced centering takes just a couple of seconds, because you have done the other forms a ton of times.
>
> With advanced centering, when you intend to get centered, you close your eyes, or look down at your spot, wherever that is, and automatically your body just releases tension because it has been trained to do that with all the repetitions. That's why you can't immediately jump to the advanced form. You need to put in those repetitions to train your body to make it automatic and fast. Advanced centering just takes a couple of seconds. You find your center, breathe, and then release tension. You're centered and ready to go.

Dylan was making good use of centering with his exceptional playing in the Hollywood studios and other gigs around LA. However, despite his success in those venues, we still had not found the root cause of his self-sabotage during auditions. It wasn't a lack of motivation or proper preparation. It wasn't an inability to focus or be in flow. I didn't think that it was his ego, id, and superego struggling with each other according to the Freudian model. I had a hunch that we should look, instead, at his personality according to the Jungian model. I thought that it might solve similar problems for Katy, Athina, and also, for me.

Jungian Psychology

Dr. Carl Jung was an eminent Swiss psychotherapist and contemporary of Freud. Although they started out as colleagues, they soon disagreed on a number of points, including about the role human sexuality plays in life. In addition, Jung developed his own unique concept of the ego. He understood the ego to be the conscious part of our mind that maintains constant vigilance about what is currently happening in our external world and internal realities. Inner reality includes an awareness of our thoughts, memories, emotions, and past experiences, as well as one's sense of personal identity.

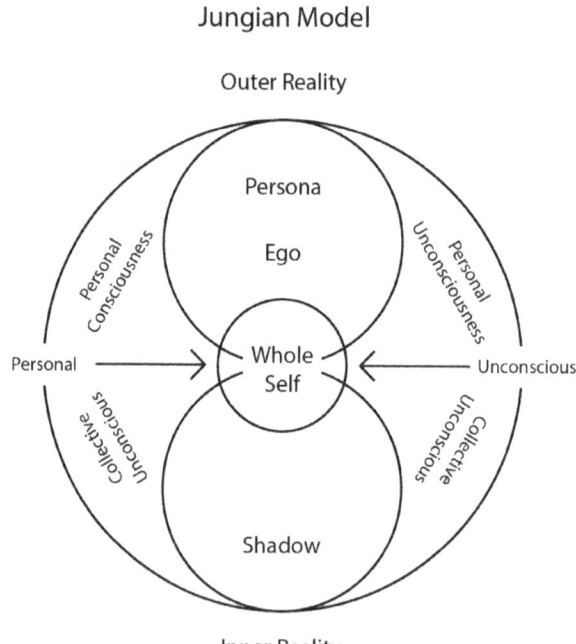

Jungian Model

The Personality

"The persona is a complicated system of relations between individual consciousness and society, fittingly enough a kind of mask, designed on the one hand to make a definite impression upon others, and, on the other, to conceal the true nature of the individual." Carl Jung

According to Jung, the ego is the "command center" of our conscious awareness. It organizes separate elements of reality, as it thinks, feels, and intuits, and as it perceives both the inner and outer worlds. Jung's model of the ego is just one aspect of a more complex and whole Self that also involves several other real aspects. These parts include the persona, the shadow, the personal unconscious, and the collective unconscious.

The persona is the mask or "outward face" that we present to the world. It is the "public relations" version of ourselves that we put on display for others to see. The persona begins to form in our childhood, when we try to please our parents, teachers, authority figures, friends, and peers. As we develop, our personas learn to show only our finest qualities in public, while concealing our less desirable features.

The shadow forms as a direct result of the persona's development. The shadow is the dark, hidden, denied, or repressed aspects of our personalities. It is the source of our basic impulses, dysfunctional behaviors, and counterproductive tendencies. These are unacceptable to our persona and frowned upon by parents, teachers, and society in general. As a result of not being allowed to engage in certain behaviors when you were growing up or forced to do things that you didn't want to do, your shadow developed its own unique preferences and separate agendas.

Unless it is recognized and better understood, your shadow or dark side will continue to adversely affect the execution of your skills, often at the worst possible times. When you recognize how this real part of your personality works against your best interests, it will lead to a dramatic improvement in your performance under pressure. Your misunderstood shadow is the primary force behind your unforced and unexplainable execution errors, especially in consequential events at critical times.

The Unconscious

"When we must deal with problems, we instinctively resist trying the way that leads through obscurity and darkness. Results can only be brought about when we have ventured into and emerged again from the darkness." Carl Jung

In Jung's model, the other main parts of your personality are the personal unconscious and the collective unconscious. The personal unconscious can be thought of as existing "below" the surface of conscious awareness. It contains all of our individual experiences, stored memories, unique narratives, and personal opinions. To access your personal unconscious, all you need to do is consider any topic. Once you do, it will open up your cache of thoughts, feelings, and prior experiences on that subject. It is always there, sitting right below the surface, just waiting for a prompt.

On the other hand, the collective unconscious is a totally different entity. The collective unconscious contains all the common instincts and knowledge that every human is born with, regardless of where and when they are born. This inherited information is shared by everyone due to our primitive past, evolution, and the repeated experiences of our ancestors. An inborn fear of snakes or spiders is an example of a universal tendency that is not learned through actual life experience.

The collective unconscious is the deepest layer in the mind. It cannot be accessed directly, but there are ways to gain access to the incredible wisdom and potential power that is stored there. That source of power can be revealed through spoken narratives, folklore, art, stories, books, plays, and movies. This process is done through the main characters in these tales, which are called archetypes.

Archetypes

"Archetypes were, and still are, living psychic forces that demand to be taken seriously, and they have a strange way of making sure of their effect." Carl Jung

An archetype is a recognizable character that holds universal meaning across cultures and times. Examples of commonly known archetypes are characters like the wise old sage, the spinster, the terrible villain, and the would-be hero. The hero is the archetype who exceeds normal limits and courageously reaches a higher level of human functioning.

The would-be hero usually starts out as an ordinary person, until she or he is called to serve a higher purpose. In order to become a real hero, they need to leave home and bravely venture into dangerous territory. An example is the main character who enters a cave, slays the dragon, captures the prize, and returns home to a hero's welcome. Joseph Campbell, who popularized the application of Jungian psychology to myths, called this adventure the hero's journey.

You have now reached a critical point on your own journey. This is where you need to summon up all the courage and willpower that you have built up till now. Make no mistake: this is not easy or pleasant for anyone, including Dylan, Katy, Greg, Athina, and me. But you must do this if you really want to move forward from here. This marks stage 7 on your adventure: the beginning of deep change.

Carl Jung was 38 years old when he confronted his own shadow. After considerable introspection, he wrote, "There is no light without the shadow, and no psychological wellness without imperfection." He considered the exploration of one's dark side to be vital for personal progress and the chance to become fully functional. Jung warned that if the shadow continues to be "repressed and isolated from consciousness, it never gets corrected."

The Shadow

"This thing of darkness I acknowledge as mine." William Shakespeare

The shadow is a very real part of our personalities that can work against our best interests. Early in our lives, respected adults taught us how we should behave, especially in public, like in school or at sporting events, concerts, plays, and religious ceremonies. By the age of five, most kids know how they should act when they are at group functions.

Through school and the socialization process, we learn the rules of acceptable conduct, mostly from adults. But our peers also set down implied behavioral guidelines for being a part of the "cool kids" or "in crowd." That group also establishes standards of dress, hairstyles, and expected opinions. Our personas try to conform to our group's implicit rules about what is and is not acceptable or sanctioned.

In the meantime, our shadows develop their own unique identities, as they oppose the personas. The identification with the personas' external personalities, and adhering to sanctioned behaviors, fosters deep-seated resentment in our shadows. They resent what they are forbidden to do or what they are forced to do. That causes negative emotions, such as frustration and anger, to begin to develop in our dark sides. The unresolved resentments then fester over time.

The shadow is the part of ourselves that we steadfastly refuse to consciously acknowledge, accept, or treat as a real entity. The shadow's alternative predispositions, scandalous desires, and questionable actions are the things that we tend to ignore, deny, and suppress. The persona tries to prevent these undesirable features from ever being seen by the world, not to mention our own conscious awareness. In the process, we turn a blind eye to the shadow's mistakes, unforced errors and dysfunction.

My Shadow

My own shadow started forming in elementary school on Long Island, New York. My father had been a Master Sergeant in the Army Air Corps. My mother was a competitive athlete. She got me into gymnastics lessons at the age of seven and swimming competitions at age eight. I started springboard diving at nine and won my first New York City championship at ten. Although I enjoyed diving and my sense of accomplishment, I was more interested in music. However, my mother, who was a controlling figure in my diving life, was not supportive of music or any of my other creative ventures.

I went to a strict Catholic high school in NY that had a top-level swimming and diving team. I was a B+ student who dove, swam butterfly, and played water polo. However, I was still fascinated with music, especially when I first heard The Beatles on TV. I used my own money to rent my first guitar, but I was never able to take lessons or practice regularly. During the school year, I practiced diving four hours each day during the week and six hours on Saturday. I finished in the top five at the national championships all four years of high school.

In my senior year of high school, I received an athletic appointment to the then all-male U.S. Military Academy at West Point. I was first-string on the Division I swimming and diving team. In the off-season, I competed in lacrosse and football in intramural competitions (referred to as "intramurder" at the academy because they were so brutal). I had not made much progress with guitar, but I still enjoyed playing in my spare time (even though I couldn't really crank up my amp in the cadet barracks!). We could not leave the military base other than on a few occasions, and we could only visit with female friends on Saturday and Sunday afternoons.

After graduation, I went through paratrooper training and Ranger School. I joined the Special Forces (Green Berets) and was selected for special agent's training in the Army's Criminal Investigation Division. After resigning my captain's commission, I became an inspector in Springfield, Illinois, investigating political corruption by state officials. Although I enjoyed the work, I did not like the cold weather. I was tentatively hired for a position with the San Diego County DA's Office. After moving to San Diego, I found that I was first on the waiting list for the next available position, but they did not know when that would be.

I had some money saved up, so I spent my time cruising around the beach, playing guitar with a garage band and volleyball with my new neighbor, Dr. Al. Al was a professor at UC San Diego specializing in psychic self-regulation, which involves consciously controlling internal bodily states. I asked Dr. Al if he knew why one of the players missed an easy shot. He gave me some books about focusing and developing the amazing powers of the mind.

I had always felt curious about why I had been so erratic as a competitive athlete, especially in high-level competitions. I could hit some of my toughest dives and then miss a simple one. It could be very embarrassing, but more importantly, it caused me to lose several important competitions. I repeatedly asked my coach about my problem, but I never got a satisfactory answer or potential solution.

When I read the first books that Dr. Al gave me, I started to finally understand some things. But despite all the reading, I still wondered about the cause of my unforced errors and bad mistakes in diving. It would take many years for me to realize that the answer lay not just in focusing better and controlling nervousness, but in a different part of my personality that I hadn't considered. I eventually came to see it as the cause of my erratic diving in competition and also of a number of other problems outside the pool.

Looking At Your Shadow

"To become conscious of your shadow Involves recognizing the dark aspects of the personality as present and real. This act is the essential condition for any kind of self-knowledge." Carl Jung

Very few people want to think about our worst parts. Jung understood the shadow to be such a reviled part of ourselves that it would only show its face as a character in dreams. We would rather not recognize our dark side as the real cause of our problems. It is easier to deceive ourselves by focusing on the best qualities and exceptional features of our personas. However, the critical first step in learning how to do better is to acknowledge your own shadow. You need to take its existence seriously, and enlist its help, if you want to create exceptional performance.

Most people have some level of awareness of their own dark side. Those who acknowledge its real presence tend to do better, especially under pressure. If you are not willing to consciously engage with your own shadow, it will continue to cause problems for you. Left to its own devices, it can result in serious dysfunction, internal distractions, an inability to focus, low energy, and other things. The unrecognized shadow creates a strong barrier between the persona and the demands of external reality. As a result, important things (like executing well in performance situations) suffer.

You need to realize that your shadow will never go away no matter what you do. You can't eliminate your dark side from your life. However, you can learn how to control it and even make good use of its powerful energy. But first you need to understand more about shadows in general. They can behave like unruly young kids who react impulsively or aggressively without thinking. As they age, they can become mean, unproductive, sarcastic, moody, sullen, irresponsible, oppositional, arrogant, purposeless, and misguided. The dark side can exhibit bad manners, use foul language, have trouble with authority figures, and struggle with unhealthy habits.

Common shadow traits include being inflexible, inattentive, cynical, vain, pompous, callous, frivolous, rebellious, inconsistent, selfish, thoughtless, annoyed, belligerent, nasty, tactless, ignorant, obstinate, irritable, pouting, unpredictable, pushy, stubborn, abrasive, devious, over-sensitive, pessimistic, judgmental, melodramatic, vulgar, quick-tempered, anti-social, withdrawn, disrespectful, self-indulgent, spoiled, temperamental, ungrateful, vindictive, uncooperative, and counterproductive.

As you see, the shadow has many faults, shortcomings, and imperfections. However, it is not entirely negative, useless, or wrong. Believe it or not, your dark side also has redeeming qualities and hidden talents that are waiting behind the persona's mask and your resentments. The dark side's powerful energy and creative abilities are hard to appreciate because they have always been ignored, neglected, or suppressed by the persona.

At first, it will be difficult to consciously become aware of your own shadow behind the persona's mask. However, if you are willing to acknowledge its real presence in your life and understand how it works against your best interests, you will be able to reach a much higher level of functioning. Do not underestimate the challenge that you will be facing though when you meet with your shadow. It is serious work that requires real effort, and you will need to lean into it.

Try to get some good sleep tonight. Stick with your routine in the morning. Spend some time reviewing all the things you've done, besides your morning routine, to strengthen your willpower. You can also look over your recent courage entries in your log. You should have noted 21 brave acts by now, especially if you played the edge and let it fly in your performances. These will all help you this week as you get ready to meet your dark side. This is not for the faint-hearted. However, if you have followed my lead so far, you will be up for the challenge.

Here are the things that I would recommend that you do today or as a part of this step:

- Practice advanced centering at least 2 times
- Maintain an optimistic outlook and positive mindset
- Continue your courage log with 3 brave acts
- Write down the things you are doing to build your willpower
- Consider your persona and shadow
- Be prepared to learn about the dark side
- Get ready for deep change
- Try to get some good sleep tonight
- Plan on following your routine in the morning

Week 3

Tuesday or Step 12

*N*ow you will learn more about the shadow, which is the dark side of everyone's personality. Most of us would rather not think about the implication that the shadow is a real part of us. It is much easier and more comfortable to read a book about someone else's dark side or watch a drama about the less attractive parts of our personalities. In many dramas, the antagonist serves as the representation of Freud's id or Jung's shadow. I recommend you check out the Billy Joel song, *The Stranger*, and see how his lyrics describe his own dark side.

Morning Routine:

✓ Wake up to energizing music

✓ Drink 8 oz water

✓ Splash cold water on your face at least 7 times

✓ Get outside within minutes

✓ Stretch and walk, bike or jog briskly

✓ Center back at home

✓ Practice mindfulness for 3 minutes

The Shadow

"The enemy is a shadow you yourself cast." Tao Te Ching

When we cannot accept certain traits as our own, we can project those things onto another person or fictional character. In the process, we fail to see them in ourselves. Think about the kind of things you find particularly offensive or repulsive in other people, or even about fictional characters. What are the things that others do that really annoy you or make you angry? This can help you catch a glimpse of your own shadow, hiding in the dark.

It's important to keep in mind that in most stories, in spite of all the despicable things that the villain did, he or she has at least one redeeming quality, talent, or capability. No human is 100% bad. Although Freud thought that people were basically neurotic, negative, and motivated only by sex, Jung had a more positive conceptualization of people and of the mind's untapped talents and capabilities that could be achieved, but only with the shadow's cooperation

I had always put off looking at my own performance deficiencies and negative tendencies until I understood. Rather than looking at my shadow directly, I started by examining my athletic persona and what I considered to be some of my best features when I was diving. That wasn't hard. As a champion diver for four years of high school, I was very confident, fearless, focused, and diligent, and I totally trusted my beloved high school diving coach. Some of the qualities I listed included:

- Confident
- Focused
- Proud
- Courageous
- Trusting

The second step in the process wasn't quite as easy. It involved thinking about the exact opposite of the persona's positive qualities. It was somewhat easier when I thought about the times when things had gone badly with my diving. After high school, the diving coach who had recruited me to the Academy was unfortunately replaced in my first semester. The replacement was someone I would never have chosen to be my coach. His coaching contributed to my being seriously injured several times, both on the trampoline and on the 3-meter springboard.

I thought back to two diving championships when I was at West Point. I had been arguing non-stop with that coach; we disagreed about everything, not just diving. I had little respect for him. I had absolutely no trust in him or his coaching. I resented him almost from the time I met him until I stopped diving. Needless to say, I didn't execute my skills very well in the important competitions. My performances were disappointing, embarrassing, frustrating, and also confusing. When I recalled those events, I realized that I had been:

- Doubting
- Distracted
- Humiliated
- Scared
- Skeptical

It was suddenly clear that my shadow's features had hijacked my persona's strengths. I finally realized why I dove so poorly in competition back then. This helped me to better understand Greg Louganis and the main reason for some of his very rare unforced errors. It happened in his first Olympics at the 1976 Games in Montreal. He was only 16. His main competition was 28-year-old Klaus Dibiasi, the "Blond Angel" from Italy who was competing in his fourth Olympics. Dibiasi was a double gold medalist on the 10-meter and current reigning Olympic Champion in that event.

Greg's coach at the time was Sammy Lee. Before he became a coach, he had also won 2 Olympic gold medals on the 10-meter platform. Now he was depending on Greg to win the gold medal and keep Dibiasi from breaking his previous record. It may sound sinister, but Greg's shadow and strong resentment against his coach caused him to make a serious mistake and lose the gold medal.

Greg won the preliminary rounds on 10-meter; Dibiasi came in second. But the points did not carry forward to the finals. Divers do 10 dives in the final stage of a competition. For the first 8 dives, Greg recalls, "Dibiasi and I were matching each other dive for dive. We only had two more dives to go, and as long as I didn't blow a dive, I stood a chance of beating Klaus for the gold. My ninth dive was a front three-and-a-half pike. For some reason, as I was stretching for the water, I kept my head down, so it washed over. I went past vertical. I got between 4's and 6's on the dive, which effectively knocked me out of the competition for the gold."

Greg knew that he, or his shadow, had done a bad dive. If there was any question though, his coach erased that. By the time he got out of the pool, his coach was cursing at him. "He called me a *dummkopf*, saying, 'Goddamnit, you're so stupid. How could you do that?' I was humiliated." His coach told Greg that he'd let him down and let Dibiasi break his record. Greg's persona didn't duck his head and miss the ninth dive; his shadow did that, using all the built-up resentment about his abusive coach.

In my case, I was presenting my work at master classes, seminars, and workshops. I found that when the event was set up correctly, my persona did really well. There was little or no interference from my dark side. As far as I knew, my shadow wasn't even waiting in the wings. For those occasions, I would list my best performance qualities as:

- Punctual: starting and ending on time
- Confident: in my professional talents and abilities
- Enthused: about the topics that I was about to present
- Focused: on my mission to give my best to my audience
- Effective: in what I was capable of sharing

When everything was ideal, the presentations always went very well. However, I remember my first presentation on Peak Performance at the Colburn School in LA. I arrived an hour early to set up my computer and test the sound system. I also met with the president of Colburn for the first time. I viewed my presentation as an audition for a potential faculty position at the school.

I felt very confident. I had given similar lectures at schools like Juilliard, the Manhattan School of Music, Oberlin, Yale, and Northwestern. I felt enthusiastic about presenting my information to the musicians, teachers, and parents who were already lining up in the hallway. But there were problems hooking up the computer to the sound system. Ten minutes before I was supposed to start, they asked if I could do my presentation without the PowerPoint. I told them that I would just wing it. As an adrenaline junkie, I usually enjoy doing that, but not when it was the first time presenting at a school where I hoped to teach.

About 15 minutes later, we finally got everything working and opened the doors. After everyone was seated, the president apologized to the group and then introduced me. He seemed very embarrassed, and rightfully so. This was supposedly a premiere conservatory, but it had taken over an hour to get the sound system to work in one of their main concert halls. We didn't have the time to do a sound check before the people started coming in. As I finally got up to speak, I knew that these were extremely suboptimal circumstances. My best qualities started shifting towards deficiencies before I ever started my performance:

- Punctual: I started my presentation later than planned.
- Confident: I doubted whether the sound system would actually work.
- Enthused: I felt anxious, rather than enthused.
- Focused: I was distracted away from my presentation topic.
- Effective: It was not even close to my usual standards.

When I finally began, I got off to a poor start. I wasn't centered. In the midst of all the chaos and confusion, I forgot to center before I began. I should have done it in the wings while the president was talking. He apologized for the technical difficulties and then made some other remarks. The only thing that I remember was right before he finished the introduction, my adrenaline kicked in with full force.

I stepped to the podium feeling a powerful surge of energy, and I thought, "Wow, I haven't felt that in quite a while." I smiled, looked out at the audience, and then fumbled my opening lines, which usually came out just fine. "Thanks, shadow, for making a great first impression," I took a deep breath and smiled again. I paused and then started my high-energy presentation. It went okay, except for the unforced error at the start.

In retrospect, I realized that my shadow had taken over the show for a few important moments. Because of the stressful situation, I was feeling really nervous about choking with a potential train wreck. I was also frustrated and angry about the unfortunate circumstances playing out in front of me. I had a hard time putting on a happy persona face. Uggh.

Carl Jung was 38 years old when he confronted his own shadow. After considerable introspection, he wrote, "There is no light without the shadow, and no psychological wellness without imperfection." He considered the exploration of one's dark side to be vital for personal progress and the chance to become fully functional. Jung warned that if the shadow continues to be "repressed and isolated from consciousness, it never gets corrected."

Here's how the French horn player Dylan described the experience with his shadow. "I had an awareness that I was holding myself back in auditions, but I didn't realize the severity with which my shadow was taking the reins. I think that's the biggest thing I took away from my work with Don over the last several years. It took me a few times to deal with the shadow, because if you don't understand the mind, or at least the self, then it's kind of hard to grasp. But once I really understood it, it made a lot of sense to me."

Katy spoke reflectively about her experience with her shadow. She also found it helpful to frame the experience as a dialogue. "I actually just talked to it, and said, 'Hey, what do you really want?' I found out that it just wants to be heard. It was just like a part of me which had been shut off because either I thought it wasn't acceptable, or I've been told it was acceptable, or I was fearful that it wasn't acceptable. I was fearful that if it came out, it would only ever cause bad things, and therefore it should just stay away. But it was just always there below the surface."

When she finally sat down and talked with her shadow, asking it who it was and what it wanted, it looked scared. "It looked like it had this anger, which was afraid behind it. It had this fragility to it, which was just kind of fearful. It's almost like it just wanted a hug, like it wanted to be soothed. It wanted to be told that everything was all going to be all right, that it didn't need to hold this anger and fear anymore because now it knew that what it cared about wasn't a bad thing."

Katy had come to realize that for her, the shadow was her fear of being too selfish or too aggressive. "I started seeing my shadow as being too overconfident, too lazy, but all of these are based in fear. Just talking to it and saying, 'Hey, what do you want?' I let all these things come to the fore. It was just like this poor little child who was never properly spoken to and never, ever heard."

Another client of mine has a very telling story about the role the shadow can play in one's life. A few years ago, I was working with an undergraduate string player at a major conservatory. Jason (not his real name or exact circumstances to protect his identity) and I had all our one-on-one sessions on Skype. Jason loved his new morning routine and got back to jogging. He said that the routine got his day off to a great start. Before long, he was making great progress in lessons, concerts, and auditions. As a junior, he won a principal position with his school's prestigious orchestra.

Jason was handsome, personable, respectful, soft spoken, and always smiling. He seemed to be very happy or at least, his persona always had a happy face on. He was a highly gifted musician who had also shown great promise on the baseball field when he was growing up. Jason and his parents, who were Wall Street investment bankers, lived on New York's exclusive and prestigious Upper East Side.

In one of our later sessions, I casually brought up the subject of resentment with Jason. I asked him to think about his past to see if there was anything that he had reason to resent. Until then, in our time together, he was always relaxed and serene and seemed to be in a delightful mood. But the mere mention of resentment caused an immediate and powerful explosion, like I'd never witnessed with any of my other clients.

Jason leapt out of his chair, screaming, and cursing at the computer, yelling something about baseball when he was young. Playing shortstop for the NY Yankees in the major leagues had been his long-cherished childhood dream. However, playing a classical instrument in a symphony orchestra was his parents' idea and their main priority for him.

His parents had hoped to be professional musicians themselves but had ended up as Wall Street bankers. They had fallen into the trap of expecting their child to fulfill their unrealized dreams. Because of this, Jason's shadow obviously still held a great deal of resentment that I did not anticipate. I was blown away. That's when I decided to write about the shadow to help others besides Jason deal effectively with their dark sides and come out successfully on the other side.

Hopefully, you'll be ready to start the process as soon as possible. You will need to conceptualize and then confront some of the worst parts of your personality. It's time to face the truth about yourself and what's holding you back with radical honesty. It's not easy, but it's not as tough as dealing with the assorted problems caused by your shadow. If you don't shine some light on its motivations, it will just continue operating in the darkness. It takes willingness to observe and fully understand your own shadow, its long-standing resentment, and dysfunctional behavior.

Plan on paying close attention in the next step to learn about your shadow's resentments. Act as if you don't know much at all about the negative things that you'd much rather ignore. Make no mistake, this can be an unpleasant process for folks at first. The shadow is what keeps so many people from realizing their full potential and achieving peak functioning.

Here are the things that I would recommend that you do today or during this step:

- Practice advanced centering at least 3 times.
- Continue your courage log with 3 brave acts
- Write down the things you are doing to build your willpower
- Get ready for the start of the deep change
- Admit that your shadow is real
- Be prepared to learn about your dark side
- It's really not *that* bad, just misunderstood and resentful
- Try to get some good sleep tonight
- Follow your routine in the morning

Wednesday or Step 13

*Y*ou will soon be meeting with the darkest side of your personality, the part that's been sabotaging your best efforts and preventing you from reaching your highest level of functioning. Hopefully, by now, you feel that you have the courage and willpower to consciously confront your own shadow. Taking this important step signifies the start of the eighth stage in your hero's journey, known as the ordeal. You can start the process by considering your own performance persona after your morning routine.

Morning Routine:

- ✓ Wake up to energizing music
- ✓ Drink 8 oz water
- ✓ Splash cold water on your face at least 7 times
- ✓ Get outside within minutes
- ✓ Stretch and walk, bike or jog briskly
- ✓ Center after you get home
- ✓ Practice mindfulness for 3 minutes

In your journal or notebook, list the top five qualities or traits that have helped your persona perform your best in the past. In your mind, go back over the best performances in your life and describe the attributes that caused you to be so successful on those occasions. Here are some of my persona's qualities that are normally associated with success:

- Hardworking
- Organized
- Dedicated
- Careful
- Resilient

After listing your own top five, consider other times when things did not go so well for you. Better yet, think about total disasters when nothing seemed to go right, both before and during your performance. It may be difficult for you to conjure up these painful memories; most likely, you would rather forget them. However, when you are able to bring them into conscious awareness and look at them, you will get a glimpse of your shadow.

Your Shadow

"There is no light without shadow and no psychic wholeness without imperfection. To round itself out, life calls not for perfection but for completeness; and for this the "thorn in the flesh" Is needed, the suffering of defects without which there's no progress and no ascent." Carl Jung

To bring the shadow into clearer view, recall the emotions that you experienced back then. These could include high anxiety, frustration, anger, or resentment. These feelings allowed your shadow to assume temporary control over your physical actions without your conscious awareness. That is when the shadow can cause considerable damage.

After reflecting on your shadow's dysfunctional behaviors in the worst possible circumstances, list the undesirable traits that accompany them. In the previous example, mine would be unmotivated, lazy, disorganized, careless, and giving up. It is not easy to admit that such things are a real part of you. However, this is a necessary step in resolving your underlying performance issues. Write down what your shadow would be thinking in the worst possible conditions, such as:

- Lazy: I just don't feel like doing some things
- Disorganized: I don't have everything together
- Unmotivated: I'm not sure if it's worth the trouble
- Careless: I'm more of a "hang loose" kind of performer
- Quitter: If it doesn't work after a while, I give up

After you capture those thoughts on paper, you will start to reveal your shadow, as you begin to take its real existence seriously. You will also start to consciously understand the source of your self-sabotage. If you want to solve those problems and achieve peak functioning, you need to have a meeting of the minds with your own shadow in order to understand it better.

As Jung explained, "Until you make the unconscious conscious, it will direct your life and you will call it fate." The persona and shadow are the pairs of opposing forces in our personalities. They are the yin and yang which represent the duality of our human nature. Your shadow, and everyone else's, seeks to be better understood and not be judged. It craves your attention and recognition. It desperately wants to be heard. If you are still making unforced errors and mistakes without knowing why, you have managed to suppress, deny, and disown this part of yourself.

Continuing to deny and ignore its real presence can result in more serious problems than occasional mistakes and unforced errors. These may include depression, self-loathing, anger, rage, high anxiety, addictions, self-deceit, psycho-somatic illness, and other symptoms. Unless you spend conscious quality time getting to know your shadow and understanding what it really wants, it will find ways to make you aware of its existence. It will continue to resist and oppose your best interests until you address and resolve its issues and resentments.

When you're ready to start the challenging work, set up your first real meeting with your dark side. There's no easy way to do this or get around it, but if you do it right, you'll soon realize that it's absolutely worth it. There are truly wonderful things awaiting you on the other side once you come to terms with your shadow.

If the process is not gut-wrenching at times, you're probably not doing it right. The shadow can be brutally honest. You will need to allow yourself to feel and accept whatever you'll be learning and experiencing in the sessions. Be prepared for some real surprises. You may cry, laugh, get angry, or feel regret. You may feel grateful and eventually joyful. In the meantime, get prepared for an exciting roller coaster ride of deep insights and strong emotions, with a light at the end of the otherwise dark tunnel.

Resolve ahead of time to be absolutely honest with yourself and unconditionally accept what you may find before you ever venture into the darkness. You will be addressing your deepest fears and worst qualities. When you first shine the light of your conscious awareness on them, you will see that they are not very pretty. Before you start each session, make sure that you feel energized, alert and ready. Find a quiet place where you will not be disturbed for at least 20 minutes, where you can sit comfortably. Turn off or silence your phone and other electronic devices. Have your pen and a journal or notebook nearby.

Meeting Your Shadow: Session 1

1. Get centered.

2. Sit quietly for at least one minute to clear your mind. Become open-minded, tolerant, inquisitive and non-judgmental.

3. Get in touch with your compassion. You want to avoid approaching your dark side with anger, blame, guilt, or shame, which could cause even more resentment.

4. Express your sincere appreciation to your dark side for being willing to meet with you. This is not necessarily what your shadow likes to do.

5. Ask your shadow what it likes to be called.

6. Inquire what it was not allowed to do, but really wanted to do. List these repressed desires in your journal or notebook. Your dark side probably still resents these things.

7. Ask about the things that it had to do but did not want to do. Your shadow may still harbor ill-will about these activities.

8. Make sure to write down everything that you learn in complete detail. It's not enough to think that you already know about these things, you need to capture them on paper.

9. Express your genuine appreciation to your shadow for sharing its unique perspective, thoughts and emotions.

10. Explain that you would like to have a follow-up session soon, after you recover from this first session. It's usually the toughest one. Then you'll be ready to reach a deeper understanding of your dark side's perspective and why it thinks, feels, and acts the way it does.

In the meantime, there are several things I would recommend that you do later today or during this important step:

- Practice advanced centering at least 4 times.
- Maintain an optimistic outlook and positive mindset
- Continue your courage log with 3 brave acts
- Write down the things you are doing to build your willpower
- Review the notes from your shadow session
- Try to get some good sleep tonight
- Follow your routine in the morning

Thursday or Step 14

*W*hen you have recovered from your first shadow session and have sufficient energy, do a follow-up session with your dark side. You need to see things from its perspective, especially its lingering resentments. Since your next live performance event is only a few days away, today we will also be covering the importance of sleep and rest. That's because your energy level can have a significant effect on your focus, state of mind and level of execution in your performance.

Morning Routine:

- ✓ Wake up to energizing music
- ✓ Drink 8 oz water
- ✓ Splash cold water on your face at least 7 times
- ✓ Get outside within minutes
- ✓ Stretch and walk, bike or jog briskly
- ✓ Center after you get home
- ✓ Practice mindfulness for 3 minutes

Resentment

"There's no birth of consciousness without pain." Carl Jung

First, I want to share with you a few of my own dark side's unattractive features. When I consciously looked at my shadow, I noticed that certain dysfunctional tendencies surfaced when I was under high stress, in less-than-ideal conditions, or in situations that I didn't like. I realized that those were the times when I became:

- Lazy
- Disorganized
- Unmotivated
- Careless
- A quitter

The next step in the process for me was gaining a better understanding of how these traits developed. I started with the first one, namely about my being lazy. Although I was somewhat reluctant to do it, I took out a legal pad and pen and got ready to ask my shadow to tell me specifically about being lazy. Although I feel that I have worked really hard for most of my adult life, I am lazy about doing certain things, like making beds and shining shoes.

Thanks to spending years at the Military Academy making hospital corners and spit-shining shoes, my shadow was evidently still resentful about those disdained activities. That explains why I have refused to shine my shoes and make my own bed ever since the day I graduated from West Point. I'm still lazy about doing those things. I usually don't translate that into being lazy in my professional life. However, when I stay at a friend's house, I manage to make the guest bed. But I will never make hospital corners or shine shoes again in my life. Now I finally understood why.

Seeing Your Shadow: Session 2

Now you will continue learning more about your dark side. Once again, make sure that you feel energized and alert before you start the session. Find a quiet place where you will not be disturbed for at least 20 minutes, and where you can sit comfortably. Turn off or silence your phone and other electronic devices. Get your pen and a journal or notebook ready to take down crucial information. Place an empty chair across from where you are sitting.

1. Get centered.

2. Sit quietly for at least one minute to clear your mind.

3. Become open-minded, tolerant, inquisitive and non-judgmental. Get in touch with your compassion.

4. Then invite your shadow to sit down across from you.

5. When you can imagine your dark side sitting there, address it by name. Express your appreciation for joining the meeting and allowing you to see it more clearly. It does not necessarily like to be seen.

6. What is your dark side wearing? How would you describe its hair and facial features? What are the expressions on its face? What emotions do they seem to convey? What does its body language say to you? Are its arms or legs folded or crossed, as in resistance or defiance? If so, ask it why it resists and goes against your best interests.

7. Ask your shadow to describe being unable to do what it really wanted to do or was forced to do what it didn't want to do. Have it describe any other unfortunate things that happened when you were growing up that caused serious resentment and bad feelings.

8. Allow time for your shadow to respond in its own way, not with the language of your persona. Listen carefully to the words and

tone. Let your dark side express its unfulfilled desires, ignored preferences, and denied presence in your life.

9. Consciously recognize your shadow and acknowledge the suffering it has experienced in your life. Capture the vital information in writing using the shadow's words, images, and expressions.

10. Thank your shadow again with genuine appreciation for meeting with you and revealing itself to you. Again, recover from this session before the next one is a few days.

Thinking back on his work with his dark side, Dylan said, "I started dialoguing with my own shadow. I spent some serious time in self-reflection where I separated my persona, my shadow, and my true inner being. I had to understand what my shadow was resenting or wanting but not getting, because that's what was holding me back in auditions."

Dylan was finally coming to understand why he could never seem to win a big audition, in spite of his impeccable practice habits. "The audition preparation process takes a long time, a minimum of one month and maximum of many more months, depending on how you prepare. That's a lot of deprivation of desire, so to speak. After all this time ignoring your shadow and pushing it aside, and pushing it aside, it may be like, 'No no, it's time for me, I'm not being pushed aside anymore.'"

Dylan was getting a better understanding of his shadow and it resented not getting what it wanted, which in Dylan's case were various activities that it wanted to indulge in, like being lazier or playing video games. He began to realize how the shadow's feeling of not getting what it wanted caused major resistance to his success, "If you win an audition, then you won't have time for all the activities that your shadow really wants to indulge in. You'll have all this responsibility for rehearsals and concerts, and you'll need to work hard. But when does my shadow get to shine? When does it get its moment? It doesn't, it thinks. My shadow didn't really want to win, and it tried to prevent me from winning by making me make mistakes before and during auditions."

After meeting with his shadow, Dylan started to understand how his self-sabotage had caused his past failures and losses, especially at major auditions. He realized that it would start to happen a week or so before the audition. His preparation would be going well before then, but a week or two before, he would practice differently, or stay up late. A couple of days before the event, he'd go out drinking with friends, thinking, "That's not such a big deal. I still have some time before the audition."

He realized, too, that he might stop eating as well, or he might work too hard on the music, tiring the muscles he needed for playing. Alternatively, he might stop listening to the excerpt list or stop playing mock auditions for other people. He found his shadow had a lot of different tricks it used to sabotage his performance long before he actually got to the audition.

He said that normally, "you would do whatever it takes to make you better. I realized that I just kind of stopped doing what I needed to do to win, and instead did the opposite." The effect was that when he went to the auditions, it was "not quite right." He'd lose his place in the music, which at a high-level audition was a kiss of death. He'd double guess where the excerpt was supposed to start and stop while in the audition. He'd decide not to empty the water in his horn, and there would be a gurgling sound during a particularly high or exposed passage which is distracting to both the player and listener.

On one other memorable occasion, Dylan decided that rather than arrive early, he would get to the music hall right on time. "There was traffic on the way to the venue, so halfway there, I got this phone call that they're going to move the time up. Where was I? That's an example of myself self-sabotaging because I know perfectly well that to do anything professionally, you always show up early. Being on time is considered late and I was just going to be on time."

In all of these situations, he'd do something that had the effect of not trusting his instincts. Now he realizes that all of these things were examples of his shadow sabotaging his performances at big auditions. "We all have things that we may not be proud of and trying to hide those things can be really exhausting. If you don't deal with your dark side in a healthy and conscious way, or if you don't give the shadow it's due, then it will pop its head up and prevent you from ever achieving your highest levels of success in whatever you're trying to do. Because that's what is holding you back from your best. You have to figure out exactly what your shadow wants, and what it is currently desiring and not getting."

It took Dylan a few times to deal with his shadow, because if you don't understand your dark side, it can be hard to grasp. It took him a few attempts to embrace and accept that the shadow is a real part of his personality, whether he was aware of it or not. Dylan, like many people, had to accept that, "This is not just a make-believe play game. It's not like I'm going to pretend to do this exercise and then go back to my supposed real life. No, this is your real life, the real you, not just something that you're doing, but it's difficult to grapple with its realness."

"Once I really understood my shadow and what it wanted, it made a lot of sense to me. I spent time dialoguing with my shadow in self-reflection." For the first time in his life and career, Dylan started to understand his dark side's true motivations, real desires and what was preventing him from preparing and performing his best in auditions.

As he explained, "My shadow wants playtime with video games or golf or hockey, and it wants to drink a lot of beer. It always wants more sleep. It loves being lazy or driving fast or watching movies or whatever. Eating junk food, staying up really late, and uninterrupted free time to engage in whatever." Once Dylan talked with his shadow, though, he was able to tell his shadow to simply wait, and it could get those things, if the shadow would only first cooperate with him on winning that important audition. We'll come back to that in a little while.

Katy also had a very moving experience of meeting her dark side. "I didn't know how immersive or emotionally all-encompassing it would be. I didn't realize that I would end up crying about my shadow. I think one of the things I most remember is seeing exactly what it looks like. I remember drawing it. I used to carry around its image with me. I realized that it just wants to be heard."

The shadow also was the parts of her that she felt bad or guilty about. "All kinds of things that I felt had been shut down actually had really positive desires underneath them, with a lot of energy which could be used positively," she recalled. "You're no longer shutting down that dark side of you and you can actually let it shine. I was able to let parts of myself go when I was playing music. It was a really wonderful thing."

Remember Athina? After she dealt with her anger and learned to forgive, she was ready to think about her dark side. She had never thought about that aspect of herself before, but she grasped the concept of listening to her shadow to try to understand it. "At first glance, it might look like it's something separate from me that just needs attention and to be listened to, but the more I paid attention to it, the more I became familiar with that important part of myself."

For Athina, the conversation didn't feel like the ordinary mental chatter that might take place in one's mind and which often sounds more like analyzing or criticizing herself. Her interaction with her shadow felt different:

> In the beginning, when I thought about my shadow, it was about a particular period of time in my life when I repeated a negative cycle of poor playing. I needed to understand the resentment in my life at the time. I thought back to that time and spoke to my shadow to understand myself back at that time. I tried to pay close attention and listen carefully to what the shadow had to say and see why it did the unfortunate things it had done in the past.

> I took a bunch of notes, because the moment I let it go, it was like a waterfall rushing out. A lot of things were there that needed to be listened to, but it was very abstract. There were visual gestures and physical sensations and emotions, all at the same time. There were also a lot of words and mental activity

inside my mind. I realized that there is a lot of stuff there with my shadow that I needed to pay attention to, not to mention some potentially positive qualities as well.

We will return to those qualities after we address something that almost everyone loves—including most shadows—and that is sleep. Your sleep, especially tonight, is a critical part of your preparation for your upcoming live event. With only two days to go, and a 48-hour delay in sleep's potential effects on performance, you need to know more about sleep cycles.

Sleep Cycles

"O bed! O bed! Delicious bed! That heaven upon earth to the weary head." Thomas Hood

One of the main things that keep talented and trained people from performing their best at an important event is a lack of proper sleep and rest leading up to the event. This lack causes physical and mental fatigue. The physical symptoms of sleep deprivation include low energy, body discomfort, aches and pains, daytime sleepiness, lethargy, impaired motor coordination, and slow reaction times. The psychological signs are inability to concentrate or sustain focus, confusion, inability to make decisions, poor judgment, irritability, frustration, depression, loss of personal power, and fear. As General George S. Patton said, "Fatigue makes cowards of us all."

How do you know if you are sleep deprived? Do you wake up in the morning wanting to sleep longer, or to hit the snooze button several times? After a heavy lunch, do you feel like taking a nap? If you fall asleep within two minutes of getting in bed, you are most likely suffering from sleep deprivation and are in a state of sleep debt. The remedy is to get more and better sleep. When it comes to sleep, both quantity and quality are important.

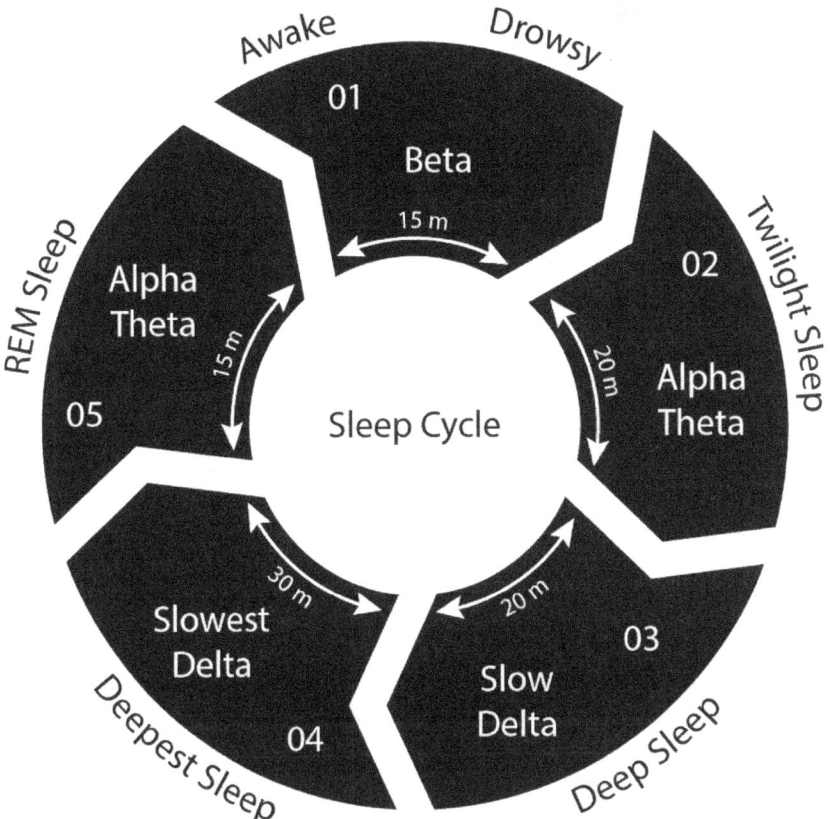

Most people cycle through five stages of sleep every night. In the first stage, people go from being awake in a high beta brain state to feeling drowsy in slower beta. In stage two, they drift off into a light sleep, known as twilight sleep. This is accompanied by alpha brain waves. In the third and fourth stages, they drift into deeper and deeper states of unconsciousness, with delta brain waves. This deepest sleep lasts for about 30 minutes, with little or no body or eye movements and the slowest heart and respiration rates.

Then sleepers start to get restless, and move around to find new positions, toward a state of wakefulness. Instead of waking up, they begin a fifth stage with faster brain waves. Their breathing and heartbeat also increase, as do their eye movements under closed eyelids, and they enter dream sleep.

In the fifth cycle, with REM sleep, the body becomes immobilized as the brain goes into alpha theta (4–7 cps). This brain wave corresponds to lucid dreams, vivid images, dramatic storylines, deep emotions, personal concerns, fears, worries, and unresolved issues. After fifteen minutes, the dreamer starts to wake up. Unless they need or want to get up, they will not fully awaken. They will slip into stage two and start another 100-minute cycle, which will repeat several times.

With each repetition, the REM period increases in depth and duration, with less time spent in the other stages. Hopefully, this week you will have five complete sleep cycles each night. Research at a sleep clinic found that alertness and focus significantly increased in adults who got eight hours of sleep. When they increased the amount to nine and then ten hours, they proved to have more energy, more accurate perceptions, and faster reactions and information processing.

Today and tomorrow are great times to work off your sleep debt with daily power naps. Try to keep these to 20 minutes in the early afternoon. Do not take them if you feel that they keep you up at night. Even a 5–15-minute nap will help recharge some of your depleted energy. However, I strongly recommend that you take a 20-minute power nap every day in the early afternoon. Power naps have been proven to increase alertness, focus, mental stamina, motor coordination, reaction times, and accuracy.

The 20-minute power nap will take you through the first two stages of the sleep cycle. You should wake up feeling alert, refreshed, and energized. However, if you sleep more than 30 minutes, you may go into a deeper sleep and run the risk of waking up feeling groggy, heavy, or disoriented.

If you can find the time in the early afternoon, I recommend that you find a comfortable place, and, if necessary, put a "do not disturb sign" on the door. If the room is not quiet, put-on noise-cancelling headphones or use ear plugs. Darken the room. Turn off all your electronic devices, other than an alarm set for 20 minutes. Center yourself. Quiet your mind and let yourself drift off.

Get up and move as soon as you hear the alarm go off. You should feel much better in a few minutes, with an extra burst of energy, refreshed and ready to move ahead. If you haven't been getting a total of eight hours of sleep a day (including nap time) in the last few weeks, please start getting more quality sleep. Optimal sleep will definitely help you in the challenging time ahead.

Here are my suggestions to get the best sleep for the next few nights, so you can perform your best in your live event:

- Refrain from caffeine after 1 pm and alcohol after 7 pm. They suppress quality REM sleep.

- Do not exercise for at least six hours before bedtime; it will keep you awake.

- Allow time to digest whatever you eat several hours before going to bed.

- Take a hot bath, which will relax you (rather than a shower, which is stimulating).

- Drink a cup of herbal tea, such as chamomile or lavender.

- Make your bedroom completely dark, with no TV or computer screens.

- Use white noise or pleasant sounds if you find it helpful.

- Cool the room to 60–67 degrees Fahrenheit (15–19 degrees Celsius).

- Decrease your physical activity at least one hour before you get in bed.

- Avoid exciting dramas or action movies.

- Read a relaxing, non-light-emitting book that you keep on your nightstand.

- Keep a pen and some paper by your bedside.

- Write down any bothersome thoughts before you turn off the lights.

In the meantime, these are the things that I would recommend that you do today or during this step in the process:

- Practice advanced centering at least 5 times
- Continue your courage log with 3 brave acts
- Write down all the things you are doing to build your willpower
- Take a 20-minute power nap in the early afternoon
- Meet with your shadow to understand its resentments
- Work on accepting and forgiving your dark side unconditionally
- Get plenty of good sleep tonight
- Strive for excellence
- Sleep in if you can
- Follow your routine in the morning

Week 3

Friday or Step 15

When you are ready and have enough energy, set up another meeting with your shadow. This time, it's about your dark side's level of involvement in your upcoming live event or performance and how you execute your skills. The goal in this shadow session is to gain your dark side's cooperation, or at least its non-resistance, in producing your best efforts. That is an important requisite in achieving peak functioning and a flawless performance.

Morning Routine:

✓ Wake up to energizing music

✓ Drink 8 oz water

✓ Splash cold water on your face at least 7 times

✓ Get outside within minutes

✓ Stretch and walk, bike or jog briskly

✓ Center after you get home

✓ Practice mindfulness for 3 minutes

Negotiation

"This process of coming to terms with the other in us is well worthwhile, because in this way we get to know aspects of our nature which we would not allow anybody else to show us and which we ourselves would never have admitted." Carl Jung

Reaching Consensus: Session 3

As always, make sure that you feel energized and alert before you start your session. Find a quiet place where you can sit comfortably and will not be disturbed for at least 20 minutes. Turn off or silence your phone and other electronic devices. Get your pen and a journal or notebook ready to take notes. As you did before, place an empty chair across from you.

1. Get centered. Sit quietly for at least one minute to clear your mind.

2. Take time to become open-minded, compassionate, non-judgmental, tolerant, inquisitive, friendly, and accepting of your shadow. Greet it by name. Express your gratitude for meeting with you. Notice how it looks and seems sitting across from you.

3. Ask your shadow if there are any other serious resentments that it has not yet brought up. If so, find out more about them and then write them down. Let it also tell you about the things that it currently wants but doesn't have or really expects to get.

4. Inquire as to whether these things are objects, like clothing, equipment, or stuff to eat or drink. They might be activities, like playing games or sports, being with friends, or engaging in creative activities. The shadow may also prefer total inactivity, as in doing nothing, just hanging out. List these things in order of your shadow's priority.

5. You need to negotiate about granting its top priorities, but they need to be fair, legal, and possible to provide within a reasonable time frame. You will grant one or more of these in exchange for your shadow's non-resistance or contribution to your performance.

6. Reach a verbal agreement with your shadow on the thing or things that it will receive after your successful event. Specify exactly what it needs to do, or refrain from doing, that could adversely affect your execution.

7. After you reach an agreement, put everything down in a written contract.

8. Sign and date the contract. Let your shadow sign it with its own name and style.

9. After the contract is signed, thank your shadow for meeting with you.

10. Following the successful performance, you must come through with your part of the agreement, delivered on time.

Here's what Athina recalled about her meeting with her shadow, "Asking for its cooperation empowered me to combine its energy with my skills and use them to produce our best mutual effort and outcomes. At the time, I was doing a lot of recording sessions in the studio, which was something that I had been struggling with in the past. I started doing more of those conversations with my shadow, trying to listen to it more and more. I found that it talks to me with more visual elements or other physical sensations as well as verbal thoughts." The more she dialogued with her shadow, the better and better her recording sessions turned out. She was sounding the best of her life. Both Athina and her shadow were happy for the change.

Tapering

After you meet with your shadow, the best thing you can do today as part of the tapering process is to relax your body and mind. Other than doing one of two mental rehearsals of your ideal performance tomorrow, try to take it easy. You should consider watching a comedy or inspirational movie, sitting quietly in a peaceful location, or getting some couch time. If the weather permits, take a leisurely walk where you are surrounded by nature, perhaps on a hike, in a park, or at a botanical garden.

Walking in nature provides a right-brain sensory experience and contrasts the left-brain cognitive exercise that you get in the polluted environment of schools, stores, restaurants, and workplaces. Hearing birds in the trees, smelling pleasant aromas in lush gardens, and seeing nature's beauty can bring a peaceful state of mind and a feeling of emotional well-being. If you live in a cold climate and it's winter, if you're dressed warmly, getting outside into the natural world will still be beneficial. Studies have shown that walking among trees significantly lowers blood pressure, anxiety, and stress levels.

Taking a walk in nature replenishes the body's cells with negative ions. When our cells are healthy, they are charged with more negative ions than positive. The positive ions have unpaired or insufficient electrons, so they carry a positive charge. These positive ions are known as free radicals. They steal electrons from healthy cells. This causes cell damage and affects our immune systems, emotions, energy, cognitive functioning, and coordinated movements. The best place to take a walk is near a body of water that is in motion. This could be by a river, stream, ocean, or waterfall. The aerodynamic movement breaks up the water drops which releases the negative ions into the surrounding atmosphere. They are like feel-good vitamins floating in the air.

If you can't make it to the woods or a waterfall today, there are several things that you can do at home to make you feel better. Listen to your favorite music or watch comedy movies that will improve your mood. For the rest of today, focus on your taper, take it easy, and get more R&R. Besides going into your upcoming performance fresh and rested, you need to be in a great mood. Today is a great day to drink extra water. Smile and flood your nervous system with happy neurochemicals.

Smile

"The real man smiles in trouble, gathers strength from distress, and grows brave by reflection." Thomas Paine

One thing that will keep your mind in a happy state is to smile. Even if you're just faking a smile, the physical act of smiling has the same mental effect. This simple act can trick your brain into believing that you are happy. Countless studies have proven that smiling relaxes the body and elevates mood states. So, practice your smile today. You get extra value if you show your teeth. It works even better when it's genuine, with thankfulness about your opportunity tomorrow to achieve peak functioning.

If your performance is in the morning, I suggest that you get up plenty early. You don't want to rush after you wake up. In fact, you want to move slowly, talk slowly, eat slowly, etc., after you get up, because you'll be feeling the extra energy. If your performance is in the afternoon, feel free to sleep in or snooze as long as you'd like. However, regardless of when you get up, you will still need to slow everything down as you go about your morning routine and other activities before the performance.

Try to get to bed around the same time as you did for the last few nights. Follow whatever routine that helps you to get a night of quality sleep. Do not turn on any lights or get out of bed other than to go to the bathroom (which you can hopefully find without turning on any bright lights). If you do not fall asleep after 15 minutes, just lie there and try to get as comfortable as possible. If you lie in bed comfortably, you can get 70% of the value of rest without being asleep. Quiet your left-brain thoughts. Imagine sitting by a waterfall or floating in a canoe on a calm lake looking up at the stars. Or imagine yourself lying in a hammock swinging gently in a dark room. Remember some happy times in your life. Instead of counting sheep, count your many blessings until you drift off into twilight sleep. Shhhhh!

In the meantime, these are the things that I would recommend that you do:

- Take a 20-minute power nap in the early afternoon
- Meet with your shadow to understand what it currently wants
- Negotiate an agreement of cooperation with your shadow
- Sign the document
- Taper for the rest of the day or step

- Take a long walk, hopefully in nature
- Smile and keep in a good mood
- Get a good night's sleep tonight
- Follow your routine in the morning

Saturday or Step 16

Morning Routine:

✓ Wake up to energizing music

✓ Drink 8 oz water

✓ Splash cold water on your face at least 7 times

✓ Get outside within minutes

✓ Stretch and walk, bike or jog briskly

✓ Center after you get home

✓ Practice mindfulness for 3 minutes

I hope that you got some great sleep last night. Today, or in this step, you will have an opportunity to execute your skills at your peak level of functioning. You can also try out the new approach to performing with your shadow's cooperation, or at least its non-resistance to your best efforts. After your morning routine, do at least one mental rehearsal session of all the important aspects of your ideal performance. After that, trust yourself, your talent, and your training to courageously go for it and let it fly!

No matter what may have happened during the performance, take a break for at least 15 minutes. Go outside, take a walk or jog, and get some fresh air. Gain some perspective before you evaluate your execution. I can guarantee that it wasn't perfect; it will never be, but I'm sure that there were many excellent moments. When you're ready to evaluate your performance, take out your journal or notebook. Rate your overall performance on a scale from 1 to 99. Then have a meeting with your shadow.

Centered _____

Positive mindset _____

Confidence _____

Courage _____

Focus _____

In flow in the zone _____

Execution _____

Shadow Debriefing: Session 4

1. Get centered. Sit quietly for at least one minute to clear your mind.

2. Take time to become open-minded, compassionate, non-judgmental, curious, tolerant, friendly, and accepting of your shadow.

3. Envision your shadow sitting in front of you.

4. Greet it by name. Express your gratitude for meeting with you, this time to gain perspective on the positive aspects of your combined performance.

5. Ask your shadow about all the things that went well in your execution. What did they feel and sound like? What did they look like, from both inside and out?

6. What were the main reasons why the shadow thinks it went well? Write it all down.

7. Inquire specifically about what it refrained from doing before or during your performance that made it successful. Take notes.

8. Explore all the helpful things it actually did to contribute in a positive way to your combined success.

9. Thank your shadow and make sure that you fulfill the terms of your agreement on time.

10. Plan on discussing any flaws that occurred in your performance in your next session with your shadow. Try to take the rest of today and tomorrow off to recover your energy.

Week 4

Monday or Step 17

Morning Routine:

- ✓ Wake up to energizing music
- ✓ Drink 8 oz water
- ✓ Splash cold water on your face at least 7 times
- ✓ Get outside within minutes
- ✓ Stretch and walk, bike or jog briskly
- ✓ Center after you get home
- ✓ Practice mindfulness for 3 minutes

Congratulations on making it to this point. You're on the home stretch, with hopeful light at the end of the dark tunnel. This week you'll continue to work with your shadow, and spend a lot more time tapering, which means backing off from intense work. You'll find fewer exercises this week, but more opportunities to see how my clients, whose stories you've been following, approached their final performances. Today's agenda also includes centering up and peaking for your final live performance event in this program. But first, we'll start with any parts of your last event that didn't go well.

Can you remember what was going on right before the mistakes happened? What was happening in your mind at the time? How did your body feel? Was it tight anywhere? Were you distracted by anything? If so, what? If you were feeling anxious, what were you fearing in the moment? If you still haven't figured out what caused your failure, I recommend that you consult with your shadow to gain a different perspective.

"The events we bring upon ourselves, no matter how unpleasant, are necessary in order to learn what we need to learn; whatever steps we take, they're necessary to reach the places we've chosen to go." Richard Bach

Shadow Reconciliation: Session 5

1. Get centered. Sit quietly for at least one minute to clear your mind.

2. Become open-minded, compassionate, non-judgmental, curious, tolerant, friendly, and totally accepting of your shadow.

3. Envision your shadow sitting in front of you. Greet it by name. Express your gratitude for meeting with you, this time to gain perspective on the negative aspects of your combined performance.

4. Ask your shadow to identify all the things that didn't go well in your execution. List them. According to your dark side, what were the main reasons for the unforced errors that happened? Did it have any involvement in causing them?

5. If so, ask why is it still resisting your best efforts? What is it trying to tell you or show you that you're not understanding? What is it that it wants, but is still not getting? Pay close attention to the answers that you're given without blame, condemnation, guilt, shame, recrimination, or further resentment.

6. Make sure that you clearly realize what your shadow has been trying in vain to express to you. You must come to understand all the reasons for your shadow's anger, rage, feelings of inferiority, sense of unfair treatment and resentments, or any other issues.

Then you can begin healing the wounds and pain that it endured using the power of your forgiveness.

7. You need to start the critical process of forgiving your dark side unconditionally, no matter what may have happened in the past. Forgiveness will help you shed the burden of unresolved anger and the heavy weight of deep-seated resentment.

8. In your journal or notebook, write a letter to your dark side apologizing for all the hurtful, unkind, unfair, and ignorant things that were done to it in the past. Keep in mind that they occurred without your full awareness.

9. Ask for your shadow's forgiveness. Neither one of you understood what was really happening at the time. Write letters of forgiveness to your dark side, as well as your persona, to begin bringing the light of conscious awareness, compassion, and healing to your entire being.

10. Write out a list of things that you will consider offering to the shadow to make amends. Then start the process of negotiating another agreement. Determine what is reasonable, not too expensive (or illegal), or will not take an excessive amount of time, in order to gain your shadow's cooperation.

Besides taking these important steps, you can express forgiveness for both your persona and your shadow, with an ancient Hawaiian prayer, known as the Ho'oponopono method. The mantra is:

I'm sorry, please forgive me, thank you, I love you. Please forgive me for holding onto the situation for so long. Please forgive me for any part I played. Thank you for the lessons you've taught me. I love you.

Say this aloud several times a day until you've reached conciliation with your dark side. This will bring cooperation and even more wondrous benefits and gifts.

If anyone knows something about forgiveness, it's Olympic diver Greg Louganis. Greg's tragic early life, both in and out of diving, is well-documented. He was physically, mentally, and emotionally abused by his stoic and angry stepfather, who ignored him until he realized the child's potential talent.

Greg was bullied in elementary school and was beaten up a lot. He was called all sorts of names. The other kids teased him because of his Samoan ancestry, his interests, and because he was shy, and he stuttered. One of his teachers called Greg a "retard" because he struggled to read. (As it turns out, Greg was dyslexic, but it was undiagnosed at the time.) Greg tried to commit suicide twice before he was sixteen. He was later raped and one of his lovers embezzled him out of all of his money. He lost his house. Despite all of that, he somehow found a way in his large heart to forgive everyone, including himself.

"The sooner you can let the victim mentality go and cross over to being a survivor, the better. But if you continue hanging onto a survivor identity, then you're still hanging onto a piece of that victim mentality. In order to let that go, you have to get to a place of forgiveness. That means forgiveness of yourself and forgiveness of somebody that may have hurt you or harmed you." They are two sides of the same coin; you cannot move past one without moving past the other.

Even though the horrific events that Greg remembers happened to him and were scary at the time, he has come to realize that he is safe now. "I am whole, I am a whole person, and I've... gotten to a place where I forgive... And in that place of compassion, I am able to forgive... So forgive yourself, whatever has you stuck, let it go as soon as you can. Try to live a life of forgiveness and understanding, with no judgments or grudges for alleged wrongs you may have suffered. People are who they are, and people do silly, sometimes stupid things. But to hang on to that, who's continuing to do harm to whom?"

Forgiveness

"Life is an adventure in forgiveness." Norman Cousins

Let me bring you up to speed with Alexa. She was preparing to take the bar exam but had never gone through law school. Although she had studied with a qualified mentor, she was having more and more doubts about her chances of ever passing. She didn't know *what* she didn't know. About six weeks before her exam, she had hired a coach, an attorney on the East Coast who specialized in preparing candidates for the bar. Evidently, that's all this woman did. She had Alexa cramming almost non-stop with all the things she thought that Alexa still needed to learn.

With a week or so to go, I told Alexa that she needed to start tapering for the event. She needed to back off from all the intense cramming and stop taking in any new information. If she didn't know the information by now, it would only get in the way of her ability to function at her best during the exam. I told her that the only thing she needed to be doing that week was tapering and practicing mental rehearsal. That meant no more cramming, only reviewing the material she had already studied and taking daily practice exams.

Alexa said that she needed touch base with her other exam coach to find out if she approved of my idea to start tapering from this point forward. The next day, Alexa forwarded an email from her saying that after 20 years of tutoring, she knew the bar inside and out. She taught her students to memorize substantive law, criminal law, and procedure. She taught them organizing the system of American jurisprudence law, and her own system to learn the vast amounts of information effectively.

Her tutor wanted to talk to me on the phone as soon as possible. When we got on the line the next day, she fired off a volley of direct questions: "Are you an attorney? Did you ever take or pass the bar exam? Did you ever go to law school? Have you ever practiced law? I thought you were some sort of psychologist?"

I told her that I wasn't an attorney; I was a performance psychologist. I explained that I'd had success helping people perform their best on tests, including the SAT, LSAT, Second Year Medical Boards, the Series 7 Exam, as well as the bar exam in a number of states. She didn't ask anything about my background or how I helped people do well on these exams. She ended the conversation by saying that she would tell her student to ignore my recommendations about tapering. After all, Alexa still needed to learn more about things like rules of evidence, torts, and contracts.

The next day Alexa called to say that she was going with me and my program and discontinuing her work with the other coach. Now she could start into her taper, with no cramming or trying to learn new material (including torts). She just needed to review what she had already learned, take practice exams using my test protocol, and taper.

Athina, the formerly angry musician now had one week left before her final graduate recital in Finland. Like many people in the final stages of preparation before an important event, I recommended that Athina also start tapering for her upcoming big event. She resisted the idea at first. After all, she still had things that she needed to work on with her music. Fortunately, she decided to go along with the tapering program.

Here's how she described it: "There is a process of resting and recovering, as I'm also preparing mentally for the performance by doing much more mental rehearsal. I'm playing less and, but I'm also working with myself to lead towards a good outcome, using positive self-talk, physical rest, and more sleep. At the recital, I want to bring my energy up to a peak, and I can use centering up to do that. By then, it's more about surrendering to the process and letting myself access those tools when the event actually takes place."

Dylan also found centering up to be a helpful practice. "It's about bringing your energy to a high, positive state to make sure that you have your highest level of performance possible. You want to have the right amount of energy. Depending on the situation, I generally center up, because I need energy to focus. If I focus the energy, I'm going to be in a great place. I'm going to be in a positive state to give a great performance."

Centering Up

By now, you have learned basic centering, in other words, how to center down to lower your energy and increase focus. Now you will learn how to center up, so you can raise your energy on command. Even if you usually have a lot of anxiety before performing, there may be times when your energy is too low because of stress, jet lag, or poor sleep. You can use centering up when you need to get energized for the event in a short period of time, and you can use it anywhere, anytime.

After you master centering up, you will be able to raise your energy quickly before you practice, perform, or execute your skills, and you will be focused in your right brain. When you are functioning from your right brain, you can clearly picture what you intend to do, hear it just the way you want it to sound, and sense the way it feels in your body when the skill is done correctly, especially with extra energy.

Start standing with your feet shoulder width apart, a slight bend in your knees, with your back straight. Have your arms and hands at your side, with your head up. Make sure that you feel in balance. The first step is to direct your eyes to a focal point, three to seven feet in front of you. Make sure that your point is below eye level. Keep your eyes focused on that point.

The second step is to make it your clear intention to raise your energy up. Get up! Power up! If you need to, scream excitedly in your head, bringing all your enthusiasm. The third step involves taking several rapid, deep breaths, in and out through your mouth. Stop before you reach the point of hyperventilating. As you take rapid breaths, do a series of deep knee bends while you pump your fists.

For the fourth step, release all the tension from your upper body in one or two breaths. Shake it out as you breathe it out. In the fifth step, for a breath or two, sense your center, two inches below your navel and two inches into your body. Get in touch with that place. Get out of your head and into your center. Feel the extra energy there.

For the sixth step, imagine the performance going well for one or two breaths. See it the way you intend it to go, hear it the way you like it to sound, and sense the way it feels when done correctly. For the seventh step, feel the energy coming up from your center through your spine. When it reaches your eyes, direct the energy out to your focal point. Then use the energy to go for it!

Centering up

1. Focus on your point. Find a place 3-7 feet in front of you, below eye level.
2. Form your clear intent. Raise your energy. Get up!
3. Start deep rapid breathing. Do knee bends and pump your fists.
4. Drop the muscle tension. Release all the tightness from your upper body.
5. Be at your center. Get out of your head and into that place.
6. Imagine it going well. See it, feel it, hear it the way you intend.
7. Direct your energy. Let the energy flow to your point. Go for it!

Practice this form of centering at least 21 times, so you can quickly get your energy up on command, wherever you are. If you are not feeling enough energy before you execute your skills, you will have a difficult time achieving peak functioning. As always, practice centering up several times a day for the remainder of the week, especially when you are feeling low in energy, and keep notes about your experience in your journal or notebook.

These are my recommendations for you today or during this step:

- Start tapering for the upcoming event
- Practice centering up 2 times
- Hold a reconciliation meeting with your dark side
- You need to understand what caused your mistakes at your last live performance
- Start to forgive your shadow
- Say the Hawaiian mantra of forgiveness throughout the day
- Follow your routine in the morning

Week 4

Tuesday or Step 18

Now you'll continue with your tapering process for your upcoming live event. We will also be exploring some of your dark side's untapped talents, latent capabilities, and unrealized potential. We'll work with your shadow on the process of assimilation and integration into your Whole Self. Then, you can meet your golden shadow.

Before we get to that, please say the Hawaiian mantra of forgiveness and love out loud several times. Feel the words resonate within you.

I'm sorry, please forgive me, thank you, I love you. Please forgive me for holding onto the situation for so long. Please forgive me for any part I played. Thank you for the lessons you've taught me. I love you.

Morning Routine:

✓ Wake up to energizing music

✓ Drink 8 oz water

✓ Splash cold water on your face at least 7 times

✓ Get outside within minutes

✓ Stretch and walk, bike or jog briskly

✓ Center after you get home

✓ Practice mindfulness for 3 minutes

Tapering

With less than a week or so before your big event, it's time to begin the final part of your tapering. Although you may not like the idea of backing off when your performance is still not perfect, you already know that it will never be perfect. This is not the time to make improvements to your skills; now you need to increase your taper by doing less in terms of physical work. None of my clients like the concept, especially when they still have things in their golf swing, concerto, dance routines, exam study, or audition preparation that they want to work on.

Katy was one of these. She was in Amsterdam getting ready for her audition for the principal horn position with the Concertgebouw Orchestra. "Tapering is really difficult because you want to keep on working, studying the scores, writing notes about the excerpts. But Don told me that I should be taking some nice walks during the days, hopefully out in nature. And they were very wonderful. They were a way of refreshing myself, so I didn't get stuck or tired. I felt constantly refreshed instead of tired, so I felt like I was building this energy before the audition, which was great. Then I could plan on releasing it when the time came for the audition." Evidently, she timed her peak for the Concertgebouw audition just right: she won!

Music student Mia was in London in the final stage of tapering before her undergraduate final recital. She would also be auditioning for graduate programs and possible scholarships. I also needed to convince her that she needed to taper, back off from practicing and playing too much, and try to get more rest and sleep. Fortunately, she agreed.

Deborah in California was having issues with her dance partner the week before a major competition. Although she was somewhat injured, the professional from Europe with whom she danced with didn't believe in backing off from his usual intense level before events. He told her that they still had things that needed to be fixed if they were going to win.

A few days before Alexa's bar exam in Washington State, she was still not a fan of the tapering process. She felt very anxious and wanted to cram in some last-minute studying. The coach on the East Coast called me again and rattled off a list of subjects that her ex-client still needed to study. I told her that Alexa needed to get some rest and overdue sleep.

Jacqueline was in the Midwest preparing for an audition to move up to another position in the orchestra. For this second audition, there were a lot of things going on in her life that had happened and that she hadn't dealt with the first time. Her stress was bringing her energy down, but the tapering process helped her manage everything that was going on.

"I was kind of annoyed with Don because he was talking to me about tapering, and I felt like I haven't even ramped up for the audition yet. 'I can't afford to take any time off,' I'd said, but he said, 'You have to do just that.' I trusted him, but I was very annoyed with him at one point. I didn't think he really got it, but now I realize that he got it more than I did. He got it crystal clear."

Jacqueline backed off on practicing and even making the all-important reeds:

> I didn't have to worry about peaking too soon. I had to just bide my time with everything, including the mock auditions, practicing the repertoire, making the reeds, and getting extra rest and sleep. And I'm not sure how I would've survived the audition if I hadn't tapered for it. I would have been completely burned out and exhausted trying to play through the excerpts.

> As the audition got closer and closer, I started backing off and focusing more on mental rehearsal, rest and recovery, and keeping myself hydrated with good nutrition. That gave me more confidence because I felt more rested, which seems to work hand in hand with what we were doing getting ready. After the final round, I called Don and said, 'I won'. These are his favorite words he loves to hear from his auditioning clients.

"He alone has a genuine claim to self-confidence, for he has faced the dark ground of his self and thereby has gained himself. He has acquired the right to believe that he will be able to overcome all future threats by the same means." Carl Jung

I hope that you're ready to take the next step with your shadow. This is a very important moment that you have been working towards for some time. This pivotal step will bring it all together for you.

Assimilation and Integration: Session 6

1. Get centered.

2. Become open-minded, compassionate, non-judgmental, tolerant, curious, honest, friendly, focused, accepting and appreciating of your shadow. Sit quietly for at least a minute.

3. Envision your shadow sitting in front of you. Greet it by name. Smile.

4. Express your gratitude for its communicating with you and continuing to reveal itself to you on a conscious level.

5. Ask your dark side again for its forgiveness for whatever you may have done to it or allowed to happen to it.

6. Ask if there's anything more you can do at this time for your shadow. If there is, suggest how you may be able to honor that request.

7. Now you can ask for your shadow for its full cooperation in your upcoming performance and life. You can know let it become a combined and united effort rather than opposing sides working against each other.

8. Tell your dark side that you need its help to do your best. Ask your shadow to assimilate its special abilities and powerful energy into your whole self.

9. Welcome your shadow and persona as real and integrated into your whole self. The whole is much greater than the sum of its parts.

10. Embrace all the wonderful and unique aspects of your shadow, persona, and whole self as you grow together towards success in unity, harmony, and love.

Assimilating and integrating your shadow into your whole self is the seventh component of peak functioning.

Remember how Dylan spent a lot of time working with his shadow? He came to a particularly clear understanding of the parts of himself, including the persona, shadow, and true inner being. His shadow wanted to be lazy, drink beer, play video games, drive fast, and watch movies while eating junk food. He had to make a deal with all those impulses that were the opposite of his ideal self, but which were still his impulses:

> If it cooperates and contributes in a specified way, you agree to make time to do what it wants to do. Uninterrupted, guilt-free time to participate in the activities that it wants to engage in. In the meantime, it will allow me to be my ideal self.

> I finally realized that it was my shadow that used to stop me from doing the things I needed to do to achieve the success I wanted. I finally realized how it affected my playing, but it pertains to everything I did, because it changed my mental construct. I reached a much deeper understanding of my true motivations and inner drives.

> Anything that I wanted to do, any endeavor, I now had all the tools I needed to deal with my weaknesses and shadow traits. I knew what could potentially hold me back and how I would deal with it. And I know that I will deal with it effectively. If I intend to accomplish something, whatever it is, and I feel resistance or opposition by wanting to do something else, I know what's going on in my head. I recognize it immediately when I hear my shadow's voice.

He continues, explaining how meeting his shadow helps him on an ongoing basis, "Now I say, 'I hear you, but let's do that later. Right now, I really need your help with this project. We can do what you want later, after we're successful right here and now.' After I started doing that, everything I did went better. You know, not just music, but playing hockey or golf, or even playing with my son. I can stay more focused, play much better, and have more fun."

Parker, the former pro golfer, also had to address his shadow in order to move to the next stage of his career. His shadow work focused on his resentment toward former golf teachers who had once ruined his swing. He needed to forgive himself for allowing them to mess with something that was already working well, and then he was able to complete the process of integrating and assimilating his shadow into his whole self. He was no longer interested in creating peak functioning on the golf course, though. Instead, Parker needed to find a new and better source of income for him and his growing family.

The Golden Shadow

"I've learned to treat myself with a great deal of love and a great deal of respect 'cause I like me…I think I'm kind of cool." Whoopi Goldberg

Fortunately, Parker was about to get to know another aspect of his personality, known as the "golden shadow." Once he made his unconscious shadow conscious, he could bring the otherwise hidden, dark parts of his personality into the golden light of self-awareness. Once you make amends with your dark side, your golden shadow will start to share its latent talents, repressed passions, and stifled creativity with you.

You will discover the golden energy and life force within you that's been trapped for too long behind denial, ignorance, repression, and resentment. You will feel liberated, free to follow your own independent choices and trust your intuition. You will have more fun and become more reliant on your personal decisions, rather than simply following group norms. You will focus more on the present and on what you can create for the future instead of dwelling on past regrets and unfortunate missteps.

The golden shadow is the source of your previously suppressed creative energy and fount of new ideas. That is the inner treasure that's been waiting for you past the shadow's darkness. That's what Parker found after he consulted with his golden shadow on creativity. He came to discover the most creative part of his mind. He could consult with it and learn from a master teacher. No one is more creative than the golden shadow.

Uncovering your golden shadow's special talents is the reward that you receive after reaching stage 9 on your hero's journey. Parker discovered his unknown talent after he consulted with his golden shadow. He had been coaching high-level players on their short game, and he was also helping the people who had a very difficult time hitting short chip shots (the dreaded "chipping yips"). He really wanted to help people who struggled with their short game with their wedges.

Parker discovered that the players set up their wedges differently for the various shots around the green. Golfers use different types of clubs to hit the short chips (low shots), pitches (high shots), and bunker shots (from the sand traps). He would help them set up to the golf ball correctly with their hands in the right position to hit those different shots. But he couldn't be there in person for everyone, of course!

"I wondered if there was something I could do to the wedges to give the golfer some sort of a visual cue or reminder about where they need to be set up to the ball with their hands correctly positioned to hit a good shot. That's when I came up with the idea for wedges with visually enhanced alignment. I thought I could have alignment lines put on wedges, and players could look down and line up the lines. Then they would know they were set up correctly without having to think about it."

Parker really believed in his new idea, and he thought it could change the wedge market for future generations of golfers: "Lots of players, from amateurs to tour players, struggle with hitting their wedges and getting shots close to the hole. If you waste shots around the greens with poor wedge shots, it doesn't matter if you can drive the ball over 300 yards. Most of those extra shots are due to misalignment of the club at address."

First, he made some prototype wedges with the lines drawn on:

> They worked incredibly well with all the players who tried them. These were mostly tour players, but I had a few amateurs try them as well. I was convinced that one of the major golf club manufacturers like Titleist, TaylorMade, or Callaway would be interested in my new wedge design with alignment lines on the club.
>
> I decided to shoot for the stars and get in touch with the right people at Titleist, the world's number one club manufacturer. I needed to set up a meeting and make a presentation to their staff about my new wedge design. I also needed more prototypes because I couldn't just go in with only two of them. I had several more manufactured professionally. They looked awesome and I knew how well they worked with everyone who tried them. I would just need to convince the guys at Titleist that my wedges were the next big thing in golf, for both amateurs and tour players.

There were a number of things that he still had to do to move along with his new creation and ultimately get it into production. He recalls:

> I would need to hire a patent attorney and start filing for patents. Then, I needed to build a sales pitch board to successfully pitch my wedges to the largest golf club manufacturer in the world. The Titleist company, and its associated name brands like FootJoy golf shoes and golf shirts, had $1.68 billion in sales in 2019.

I was trying to figure out how I was going to sell them on my new wedge idea. All I'd been focused on for most of my life was my own golf game and my own playing career. Now I was facing the daunting prospect of selling my revolutionary design to the staff at Titleist. I needed to use the same skills that I learned from Don to win on the PGA Tour to win over the staff at the largest club manufacturer in the world.

I started with a large poster board, for planning and to capture my visions and ongoing ideas. I found a local patent attorney who filed for two provisional patents for my wedge design. I contacted a guy I knew on the professional staff at Titleist. I met him when I was playing out on tour. I called him and gave him a general idea about my new alignment system for wedges. He said he'd get back to me. I went back to my poster board.

Although Athina did not know anything about golf or wedges, she was very interested in her own creativity. "I figured out my shadow's desired reward for its cooperation is when I'm able to engage in something creative. It's like giving a child watercolors and paper. It can be so simple, but there are moments like those where I wanted to mark the accomplishment of the process I was going through by doing something creative."

Deborah was definitely in her right brain in her Spanish dance competition. Her professional partner from Eastern Europe finally backed off, at least a little. It was a good thing, because by then she had a number of minor injuries from overtraining before her competitions. Nevertheless, when the time came, they were able to get in sync and in flow, at least when they were on the dance floor. They won national titles in several different categories. She was on her way to get some very nice rewards, like a golden necklace, that she could wear when dancing in big competitions. It would serve as permanent reminders of her success.

These are my recommendations for you today or during this step:

- Increase your taper
- Practice centering up 4 times
- Assimilate and integrate your shadow into your whole self
- Review the 7 components of peak functioning
- Consult with your golden shadow
- Be open on a conscious level to its creative ideas and special talents
- Follow your routine in the morning

Week 4

Wednesday or Step 19

Welcome to stage 11 on your hero's journey, which is known as the final push. This is the last major obstacle for you to confront on your adventure before heading for home. It may be your toughest challenge yet, but there's no way around it—not if you still want to reach your peak level of functioning in your upcoming live performance.

Morning Routine:

✓ Wake up to energizing music

✓ Drink 8 oz water

✓ Splash cold water on your face at least 7 times

✓ Get outside within minutes

✓ Stretch and walk, bike or jog briskly

✓ Center after you get home

✓ Practice mindfulness for 3 minutes

Your last opponent on your trek is not your shadow, your persona, or any other aspect of your personality. This real enemy is the instinctive and natural fear of your own death. In order to complete this stage of your journey, you must face the idea of your own untimely demise. This powerful exercise is meant to help you confront the fear of your own ultimate death—and then experience a joyous rebirth.

Death and Rebirth

"Death is not the enemy, living in constant fear of it is." Norman Cousins

The next exercise will seriously test your courage and willpower—even if you have tried it or experienced something near to death before. I know this is true because I had a near-death experience after a bad accident I suffered when I was in the Green Berets. I went into a deep coma in an army hospital and came back shortly after receiving the last rites from the special force's chaplain. He welcomed me back and told me that I was very lucky. I have no recollection of being in a coma; nor did I experience what is known as a near-death experience (NDE).

However, many people who have had NDEs report similar themes and events. These include leaving the body, looking down on oneself, and being aware of other people in the room, then traveling down a long tunnel, often moving very fast toward a bright light. Many people report encountering beings of light or religious figures and then feeling comforted, with a warm sense of unconditional acceptance, peace, and love.

Almost all the subjects of NDE research describe reaching a point where they needed to make a decision about whether to stay in the afterlife or return to their bodies. With the choice to return came the realization that they had not yet accomplished important things, or they had people in their lives who still seriously needed them. Once they decided that they needed to go back, they returned immediately to their bodies and became aware of their breathing.

People who have had NDEs feel transformed by the experience. They feel happier, more relaxed, with a sense of well-being. They have a new perspective; a clearer sense of purpose, greater compassion for themselves and others, a strong desire to learn and grow, and an overwhelming sense of gratitude. Many of them report that they stop worrying about insignificant things and no longer have a fear of death.

Fortunately for you, you can experience some of these benefits by completing the following death and rebirth exercise. I did the death and rebirth exercise for the first time over 25 years ago when I was conducting golf clinics in Vail, Colorado. At the time, I was reading books about developing the powers of the mind. I worried that if I imagined my own death in complete, vivid, and dramatic detail, it might happen, but obviously I managed to survive.

The exercise opened me up to new ideas, unexpected possibilities, and a very different career path. In Vail, I met an orchestral musician who'd contacted me for help with his golf game. This chance encounter put me in touch with his orchestra, the Syracuse Symphony, and three months later, I gave my first presentation to the musicians of the Syracuse Symphony. It was well-received. Five years later, I was on the faculty of The Juilliard School, the New World Symphony Orchestral Academy, and the Perlman Music Program.

As a direct result of doing the death and rebirth exercise, I became aware that I had something unique and previously unavailable to offer to performers of all kinds, not just competitive athletes. It opened me up to a whole new and exciting world. This exercise was the first step toward my next adventure and unexpected possibilities.

Set up the right time and place for the death and rebirth exercise. Do this when you are feeling energized and alert. It will take about twenty or more minutes. You will need to be in a quiet room where you can lay down and not be disturbed. Put your journal or notebook and a pen near you. Set a timer for 20 minutes. Turn off all other electronic devices. Lie down and make yourself comfortable. Take several deep breaths. Close your eyes and relax.

Death and Rebirth Exercise

1. Summon all the courage and willpower that you have built up over the last several weeks.

2. When you are ready, imagine that you are presently at your own funeral.

3. Imagine yourself lying in a casket.

4. Accept that you are now deceased, at least for the time being.

5. Imagine everything in complete detail. Feel the coffin, hear the music, smell the flowers.

6. Think about everyone who would be there. Hear the things that they would say about you.

7. Picture your family and closest friends as they walk past you in the casket.

8. Imagine that the service is about to finish. However, right before they close the coffin, you are given the choice to move on to the afterlife or return to your life on earth.

9. You can return if you have something really important to do or complete. Something that no one else can do but you. What would that be? Dwell on these ideas until the timer sounds.

10. Reset the timer for another 10 minutes. Vividly imagine yourself bringing these realizations into form in your life. When it sounds, capture your new ideas and visions in writing.

My clients found it a powerful way to see themselves and their careers in a new light. Bart, the classical musician living in Poland, recollected:

> The death and rebirth exercise changed my life completely. I was supposed to imagine my funeral when I'm lying in the middle of the church. All my family is there around me, with all my friends saying my words about me. Everyone there's crying. It was an awful atmosphere. Then I imagined that the coffin was about to close, but then I thought about important things in my life that I hadn't finished.

I saw in my mind a view similar to what you would see in Norway, with very beautiful grass and a flowing river nearby. In the middle of the picture, I saw a beautiful sun with an eagle flying from behind me into the sun. That eagle actually changed my whole perception. Every time when I'm playing music, I feel like the eagle soaring higher and higher with my musicality. I felt lighter and free. After the exercise, my playing really took off. It was really beautiful.

Not too long after that experience, Bart won a huge audition for a major symphony orchestra in Poland.

In Amsterdam, Katy also had a profound death and rebirth exercise, but she started with some skepticism. "This is going to feel a bit weird," she thought, "but if it does work, I'll feel something, I don't know what." Eventually, she was able to completely suspend her disbelief because of the other exercises she had been working on that had helped her so much.

When she reached the rebirth part of the exercise, it was a life-changing moment for her, too:

It felt like I awoke to a different part of me for the first time, the part that was connected to everyone who had come before me. I felt grateful for my mother, my grandmother, my grandparents, and my great-grandparents. I felt like I had all of their hopes and dreams, and all of their power, all of their energy, and all of their courage that they displayed in their life. I felt like I had them all on my side and like I was part of them.

I realized that all of the possibilities of goodness and strength in the world were available to me if I chose to be open to them. The gratitude and wonder with which my eyes opened was just astonishing. I knew that anything was possible for me from that point forward. That was really special. Wanting to be open to that kind of thing, and absorb it, and hopefully release it back to others as well with love. I realized that through my French horn, I was going to create joy and beauty through sharing my sound. I'd be fulfilling my own potential and hopefully helping others do the same.

Greg Louganis also had his own experience facing mortality. At the 1988 Olympic Games in Seoul, Korea, he was on the 3-meter springboard in the preliminary round. He was doing a reverse two-and-one-half somersault. It was the ninth of the eleven dives that he needed to do in order to qualify for the finals the next day. It was one of his best and most reliable dives. I'd never seen him miss this dive. Unfortunately, this time he had a really bad accident. He recollects:

> As I was getting ready to climb the ladder, Ron was debating whether to warn me that earlier I'd been a little too close to the board on another one of my reverse dives. But he decided not to say anything, because I was never close doing my reverse two-and-one-half. My distance on that dive had always been just right, so Ron decided that he didn't want to give me something else to think about.
>
> In one of the articles published during the Olympics about my diving, the reporter estimated that I had done 180,000 springboard dives in my 18-year career. I had never, ever, hit my head on the springboard, but that time, I did. Every major newspaper published a picture of my head making contact with the diving board. It was a shocking moment, and not only for me. I was the top diver in the world, and almost no one imagined I would hit my head on a diving board at the Olympics.

Afterwards, people learned why he made the mistake. Earlier in the year, he had been diagnosed with human immunodeficiency virus (HIV).

There was no known cure at that time. The only people who knew that Greg had tested HIV-positive were his doctor, his attorney, and Ron. He had even waited a while to tell Ron about his condition and that he was on some heavy medication.

Greg's doctor put him on AZT (azidothymidine), gamma globulin and Bactrim, all to suppress disease. As he said later:

> AZT is no vitamin pill. It is strong stuff, designed to keep the HIV from completely destroying what is left of the immune system. I tried to put that frightening thought in the back of my mind, but I carried around a little alarm clock to remind me to take the AZT every four hours. It was a six-times-a-day reminder that I had a deadly disease. I also had to carry around a pillbox with lots of different compartments, for the AZT, the Bactrim, and all the vitamin supplements I was taking. Fortunately, because it's common for divers to take lots of aspirin for injuries, no one questioned me about the pills.

Ron had suspected it for some time. He noticed that Greg's moods were pretty bad and that he was having a difficult time staying motivated. Greg initially didn't tell Ron because he was afraid Ron would go easy on his training. When they finally talked about it, Greg told him, "There's no way I'll make it through the Olympics unless you treat me the way you always do. I have to go through the program as if nothing is going on, because I need the confidence I get from my training to compete at the Olympics."

"He asked me how I was doing. I tried to speak but as I started to cry, Ron came around his desk to where I was sitting, and he held me, like he always did. I calmed down." The first thing Ron said was, "We'll get through this together." Amazing words to hear from anyone.

Then he asked Greg what he wanted to do. "I want to continue", he said. Ron said I shouldn't worry about him holding back in my training because he wasn't going to let me off that easy. Before I left Ron's room, we agreed we each had a job to do. Ron said he wasn't going to neglect his part and that we all had to work together. He gave me a big hug and we parted."

Greg had the gash in his scalp stitched up, and because he needed to be alert to do the dives, he went through the procedure without any anesthetic. Greg would need good scores on the last two dives to qualify for finals the next day. Although he received zeros on his failed dives, he still had a chance if he got seven-and-a-half's and eights on the dives. Unfortunately, both dives were reverse somersaults, spinning again back towards the board. Greg got poised to do the first dive and smiled.

"People didn't realize how badly shaken I was, and it wasn't until after I completed the preliminary round and made it to the finals that I thought about it. Otherwise, I would never have made it through." He nailed the dive, as well as his reverse three-and-a-half, and made it into the finals, which were the very next day.

These are my recommendations for you today or during this step:

- Increase your taper
- Practice centering up 5 times
- Continue your courage log with 3 brave acts
- Do the death and rebirth exercise
- Get plenty of good sleep tonight
- Follow your routine in the morning

Thursday or Step 20

*N*ow, with only days to go before your live performance event, you should be increasing your taper by cutting back on physical things and doing less and doing more mental rehearsal. We will be reviewing the components of peak functioning and the importance of getting a good night's sleep for the next few nights. I will be covering normal fears and doubts, stress chemicals that are in your system, happy neurochemicals, gratitude and peaking for your big event.

Morning Routine:

✓ Wake up to energizing music

✓ Drink 8 oz water

✓ Splash cold water on your face at least 7 times

✓ Get outside within minutes

✓ Stretch and walk, bike or jog briskly

✓ Center after you get home

✓ Practice mindfulness for 3 minutes

You have now reached stage 10 on your hero's journey: the return, meaning that you're finally heading for home. At this point in your adventure, you are likely to be experiencing a rollercoaster ride of fluctuating and heightened emotions. This will probably continue for you from now until your event is over. Due to the extra stress and anxiety in the last days before consequential events, peoples' nerves often get raw. They become overly sensitive and get testy or prickly, especially around others. That's due to the fears and doubts that usually accompany big events.

Normal Fears and Doubts

"A man's doubts and fears are his worst enemies." William Wrigley, Jr

As people get closer to important performance events, their anxiety and frustration does not diminish. It increases, especially when things don't go as originally planned (which they never do). If unfortunate things happen several weeks before a big event, like an instrument or equipment needing repair, it's no big thing. However, if something needs fixing the week before the event, it can become a major thing. A Lithuanian psychologist, Dr. Bluma Zeigarnik, discovered how the mind tends to fixate on a project that has not been completed, especially if it's not on schedule. It can really freak people out. This tendency is known as the Zeigarnik effect.

Now is the time to be aware of the real potential for your anxiety, frustration and testiness around others to increase, as you get closer and closer to your final performance. For the next few days, remain on the lookout for the Zeigarnik effect and how it can make you feel. When you sense that your level of anxiety or frustration is rising and you're becoming super sensitive, recognize it for what it is. Center. Remember to keep your sense of humor. Don't get caught up in your own melodrama.

It is also very common in the time leading up to big events for people to experience significant drops in their confidence. I refer to this phenomenon as "normal fears and doubts" (or NFDs), which usually accompany consequential live performances. There is never any guarantee of how it's going to go, but it's not going to be perfect. It is normal to experience heightened fear and doubt in the days leading up to the big event. However, these normal fears and doubts are not helpful to you, especially now.

Here's an example: You're riding in your car a few days before your performance. All of a sudden, out of nowhere, you get hit with a shot of adrenaline, which I call a "zinger". It happens in a flash when you think, "What if I screw up?" or, "I'm worried about doing poorly." These zingers can zap you with an unpleasant lightning bolt of energy that can be very disturbing.

If you start thinking about not doing well in the performance, it can quickly lead you to think, "That would be terrible," or, "It would be humiliating," or, "What would everyone think?" This sort of negative progression can occur very quickly. Left unchecked, the progression can soon lead to imagining the worst possible scenarios. It may be normal, but it does not serve you in the final days leading up to your important performance.

Cue Utilization

"They who have conquered doubt and fear have conquered failure."
James Allen

When you get zapped, you might allow the progression to quickly take you to imagining the worst, or you can start making good use of the inevitable zingers as cues or mental triggers. The coping strategy for dealing with zingers and handling NFDs is known as cue utilization. It starts with the zinger and ends up with you being in a much better state of mind.

Cue utilization begins when you identify the source of the zinger as a normal fear and doubt. Just say to yourself, "Ah, a normal fear and doubt." As you recognize it and label it as an NFD, you gain distance from it. Then you are dealing effectively with it, rather than getting caught up in the middle of snowballing fears and doubts. The process of objectifying the zingers will set you up to use them as cues for producing more positive results.

When you get a zinger and imagine yourself making a mistake, go back in your mind to some of your best performances and moments of superior functioning—your own highlight films. Rather than imagining things that could go wrong, go back to times when you nailed them. Remember what they looked like, how they felt, and what they sounded like. Immerse yourself in the right-brain memory of your best performances. Stay there until you vividly recall the positive experiences.

Some of my clients found very helpful ways to cue themselves into better states of mind. Deborah started using cue words the morning of a dance performance to get her into a good mental state for the event. These weren't words that had anything to do with dance. As she said, each cue "really helps you envision a place that really makes you feel comfortable, that place that you get to when you meditate, or you need to calm yourself."

Jacqueline also found cues helpful, "One of my biggest struggles was getting me from left brain to right brain. My process cues were words or phrases that would communicate images or sounds or sensations or non-emotional feelings to my right brain and turn off my left brain. These process cues would help me immediately know what I had to do to get the effect that I wanted. They were different depending on the piece and the mood I wanted to create with the music." She used phrases and words like "sing," or "sing and dance," or "spin the air," "move the air," "clear and balanced", whatever worked for each different moment.

Keep in mind that your fears and doubts do not actually exist outside of your mind in external reality. Consider all the things that you've worried about in the past. The likely fact is that most things that you've worried about never really happened. And most of those weren't worth worrying about in the first place. If you're hit with a zinger for which you have no highlights, simply imagine whatever you were worried about going just the way you'd like, in three different and vivid versions.

The cue utilization strategy will put you in a better state of mind, because each zinger will cause you to create positive experiences in your mind. Thanks to the inevitable zingers, especially in the final days leading up to your big event, you will be afforded many opportunities to use this approach when dealing with NFDs. The idea is to get adept at using the zingers to establish a positive mindset in the next few days.

Stress Hormones

"You can't always control what goes on outside, but you can always control what goes on inside. "Wayne Dyer

You have likely been experiencing extra stress with everything you have going on, especially with your shadow work and the death and rebirth exercise. Now, it's only two days before your performance and you probably don't feel 100% prepared. Maybe not even close. This high stress sounds the alarm in the amygdala, the fear center in our brains, leading to the release of the three stress neurochemicals.

The first is adrenaline, the fight or flight messenger that instantly signals the body to gear up for action. Adrenaline increases heart rate, blood pressure, lung capacity, and blood flow to the large muscles. This can temporarily produce almost superhuman strength and power, lightning speed, fast reactions, and animal-like aggression. After the adrenaline is in the system, the brain next releases norepinephrine, another powerful substance, to better prepare the body for the anticipated physical challenge.

Finally, the third stress chemical is the steroid hormone cortisol. Cortisol works more slowly than either adrenaline or norepinephrine. Cortisol stimulates glucose production, which supplies extra energy to the body after initially encountering a threat. Cortisol is released in response to stress, worry, or anxiety, or all three. Like the other two stress chemicals, cortisol can cause real problems when circulating throughout your system, including a range of physical ailments, coordination difficulties, insomnia, inability to focus, and increased doubt, anxiety, and depression.

Happy Neurochemicals

"The happiness of your life depends upon the quality of your thoughts." Marcus Aurelius

It is highly likely that due to the additional stress you've been under lately, all three stress chemicals are floating in your body and brain these days. Fortunately, there are four neurochemicals that can counteract them and their effects on your body and mind. These happy substances are serotonin, dopamine, oxytocin, and endorphins. They all minimize the effects of high stress. In order to reach a peak level of functioning, you will need to be in a really good mood, with plenty of happy chemicals flowing in your system.

Serotonin comes from the pleasure/reward center (the nucleus accumbens) in the brain. It is released into your nervous system by exposure to sunlight and fresh air, walks in nature, sensory pleasure, fun activities, completing challenging projects, being grateful, and listening to your favorite music. When it is triggered, serotonin reduces anxiety while providing feelings of contentment, euphoria, and bliss.

Dopamine is a neurotransmitter that is released whenever you expect to have a desired experience or receive something you want, like a reward. It is triggered with the anticipation of your favorite foods or enjoyable activities, as well as feeling respected or appreciated. It is also released when you are fully engaged in highly challenging tasks that require your total and undivided attention. Dopamine makes you feel alert, focused, and happy.

Oxytocin is known as the love hormone. It is secreted by the pituitary gland in response to physical affection, pleasurable activities, massage, close personal connections with friends and loved ones, being admired, falling in love, and being in love, especially with who you are and what you love to do. Oxytocin causes a surge of positive emotions and joy.

Finally, endorphins are produced as a response to pain, discomfort, or vigorous and extended aerobic exercise. They activate the opiate receptors in the brain, causing analgesic effects, reducing stress and anxiety, increasing self-esteem, and providing a sense of well-being. Endorphins are partly responsible for the feeling of euphoria after a long workout or a deep tissue massage.

Certain scents in candles or essential oils, especially vanilla and lavender, trigger endorphins. Three small squares of dark chocolate, especially if it's more than 70% cocoa, send endorphins into the bloodstream. As you go through these next few days, you'll want to find ways to boost these happy neurochemicals—and when you do, remember to feel grateful, too, because that will also help those substances along.

Gratitude

"If the only prayer you say in your whole life is, 'Thank you', that would suffice." Meister Eckhardt

One of the best ways to boost your mood is by being sincerely grateful for all your many blessings. It is better than chocolate, since it has zero calories and zero guilt. Gratitude is a very powerful emotion and a key to achieving peak functioning in your upcoming performance.

If we don't consciously appreciate our blessings and successes, our sense of them tends to diminish or fade away. Ingratitude is often accompanied by arrogance, entitlement, an over-inflated sense of self-importance, and a skewed perception of reality. It is easy to take for granted things that we already have or abilities that we possess, until we lose them. After that, we tend to obsess on the things that we're lacking, which reinforces their absence. This can cause doubt, pessimism, and depression, resulting in additional stress and high cortisol levels. The solution is gratitude.

Some of my clients whom you have met, including Athina, Katy, and Bart, experienced a profound sense of gratitude after completing the death and rebirth exercise. It gave them an enhanced sense of thankfulness for their blessings, for the people in their lives, for their ability to perform their instruments, and many other things beyond music. Their sense of gratitude permeated their performances, and that's a good thing.

Jacqueline, the bassoonist in the Midwest, had chosen a symbol for herself as a reward for her hard work. She decided on a necklace because she would be able to wear it as a reminder. She created a necklace that had symbols of her husband and daughter so that "no matter what happened, it would always help me keep things in perspective, focused on what really matters, way more than this audition." Jacqueline literally found a way to wear her gratitude around her neck and keep it close to her heart.

When you feel thankful for someone or something, it lowers cortisol levels in your body and helps eliminate other toxins that have built up in your system. Scientific studies have proven that being grateful reduces hypertension, improves the quality of sleep, increases energy, decreases inflammation in the body, and boosts the immune system.

Gratitude actually changes the neuroplastic brain (which is a term for the way the brain can change as you encourage it to think or feel or act in new ways). Feeling appreciation wires new neural pathways to the bliss center (nucleus accumbens) in the brain, as well as reinforcing old pathways and connections to the pleasure and reward center. Research has proven that being grateful increases the amount of gray matter in the cerebral cortex, which means that you become smarter. Imagine that.

The act of expressing appreciation for benefits that you have received or of being complimented by someone (including by yourself) releases dopamine and serotonin into your nervous system. These chemicals quickly enhance your mood and make you feel happy. Sincere gratitude is a natural and effective antidepressant that also increases optimism, confidence, and self-esteem.

Thankfulness in any form for others, ourselves, successful events, positive outcomes, current favorable conditions, or even what we may not consider at the time to be beneficial, makes us feel good. The more we appreciate, the better we feel. The better we feel, the more we have to be grateful for and the happier we will become. Since it feels so good, we are motivated to repeat the process. This begins an upward spiral toward happiness.

The powerful practice of gratitude involves recognizing a personal benefit for you. Think about the desired result that you received in the past or are receiving at the present time. You next need to express your appreciation for it: verbally, in writing, or through action.

By expressing your gratitude on a daily and continuing basis, you will strengthen new neural pathways towards your bliss center. You will also strengthen the grooved connections to that feel-good, happy place in your brain. Conscious thankfulness for past, present, and future successes and rewards will cause you to be in a state of happiness and joy more and more of the time.

Appreciate and celebrate what you already have that is really good or beneficial if you want more of it. "Thank you" says that you desire to have more in the future of what you are grateful for now. If you appreciate, accept, and allow it, you will attract more wonderful things into your ongoing experience. That will support the upward spiral to even more accomplishments, contentment, and success.

After her recital, Athina had many reasons to feel grateful. She had played for the faculty panel and passed her final exam. "My graduate recital went extremely well. Even the jury members mentioned how well I played. These were people who I have worked with in the past. They have known my playing over the last five years. In their feedback, they pointed out how much I've progressed. They also enjoyed my attitude very much, as well as the music and the sound. There were a lot of good comments from these people who have listened to me in the past."

In England, Mia also focused on gratitude after several successful performances with peak functioning and flawless execution. These happened in her auditions for graduate music programs in London and Manchester. As a result, she was accepted to all the schools, including her two favorites, the Royal Academy of Music and the Guildhall School, both in London. Both schools offered her full scholarships, amazing rewards for all of her hard work!

Recovery in the Moment

"It's important to keep trying to do what you think is right no matter how hard it is or how often you fail. You never stop trying." John Wooden

Let's go back to those 1988 Olympic Games in Seoul, where Greg was getting ready for the 10-meter platform prelims. He had hit his head on the springboard only a few days before, but thought he needed to keep going and complete the work he had come there to do. His story says quite a lot about bringing your best to the fore when it really matters. I offer his words here as something to consider as you approach your own main event.

It had been five days since I'd done any training on the platform. My head still hurt quite a bit, and I thought it would hurt like hell when I hit the water. It did, especially when I missed my hands. When you do it right, you clasp your hands together just before you hit the water, and your hands break the surface, rather than your head. If your hands are apart, though, your head absorbs a lot of the impact. In the few times I missed, my ears were ringing from the pain.

By the time the platform for preliminaries began, I was feeling pretty good about diving, but I was awfully sore. I still had stitches in my scalp, and my head ached. For my bad shoulder, I needed two ice treatments every day and EGS (electro-galvanizing stimulation) to kill the pain and maintain mobility. My bad wrist had to be taped to keep a bone chip from irritating a ganglion cyst. I had sinusitis and after that one good night's sleep, I was back to being up most of the night.

The preliminaries the next day had no surprises, and Greg recalls that he got through it "basically on autopilot, and then I won. "He needed to win the prelims on 10-meter after what had happened on the springboard. "I wanted to show the judges that I was still one of the top players. I wasn't used to being beaten in the major world-class competition, and I didn't want that to happen again."

In the final dive on 10-meter though, he trailed the Chinese diver, Xiong Ni, by three points. "Ni was getting ready to do his inward three-and-a-half somersaults with a 3.2 degree of difficulty. I had my most difficult dive, a reverse-three-and-a-half somersaults, with a 3.4 degree of difficulty. As I made my way to the platform, when I was climbing the steps, I focused on my breathing, because so often when we're in high stress situations, we forget to breathe." But Greg knew to breathe, and he was also visualizing what he needed to do to be successful in his final dive.

Even so, as he waited in the stairwell just out of sight, as is courteous to the other competitors, Greg saw a flash of the other diver going by, and then he heard the rip. The rip is the sound that a diver makes when entering the water with no splash. It sounds like somebody is ripping a sheet in half. I knew it was probably like absolutely no splash at all. The crowd went nuts, cheering and clapping and stomping their feet. The sound was so loud that I could feel the vibration. I felt like it went on forever. It was crazy."

It was enough to make Greg wonder if he could pull off a comeback. It would require immediate mental recovery in that moment. We'll return to Greg's final dive at the Olympics soon, but first, I want to think through two key ideas with you a little bit more.

Flawless Execution and Peak Functioning

"Success is achieved by those who try and keep on trying." W. Clement Stone

Dylan was only two days away from his big audition for the principal horn position with the Hollywood Bowl Orchestra. It was a highly sought-after summer orchestra for musicians in Los Angeles and beyond. He had been playing the best of his life recently and we both thought that he could win it if his performance in the final round was flawless.

He had become careful to distinguish flawless execution from making no mistakes:

> I don't know any professional musicians who don't make mistakes. Whether it's a note mistake, a time mistake, or whether it's slightly out of tune, mistakes become different at this level. When you're first starting out, it's just trying to get the right notes. Then it's trying to get the right notes in the right tempo. Then it's trying to get the right notes, in the right time and the right pitch.
>
> Then it's trying to get the right notes in the right tempo with the right pitch, with the right sound. Then it's trying to get the

right notes with the right pitch, with the right sound, with the right style, and so on. So, it's hard to say that something was flawlessly executed. Being in a flow state is about as high as you can get as far as that goes, because then at least you're doing everything you possibly can do to execute to your highest level of potential, if not higher than what you're normally doing.

None of this is about being perfect. It's about being present. It's about your intentions. You basically set yourself up to achieve your intentions without getting in your own way, which will provide you with a flawless execution. It's the flawless execution of the plan. I went to the audition, I ate right. I slept correctly. I warmed up right. I didn't overdo it. I was in a great mental place before my excerpts. I flawlessly executed my plan that got me to the highest level of execution that I could get to, and that's all you can do.

He recognized that he couldn't change factors outside of his control. "Ultimately you can't decide for the committee, especially in an audition, right? Even if you didn't make any note mistakes, maybe that's not what they're looking for. Maybe they're looking for a different sound. Maybe they're looking for something else, and it doesn't really matter, 'cause you can't control that. Right?" If you do make a mistake, "It's about not allowing those mistakes to change your plan of execution. And that's what flawless execution is."

Peak functioning follows from flawless execution. As Dylan says, "it is when you are flawlessly executing your plan and everything just kind of happens. It's being in that state of flow, not getting in your way mentally, allowing your body to do all of the things that it knows how to do. Excess mechanical input will pull you right out of peak functioning."

Dylan won the audition and the coveted principal position with the Hollywood Bowl Orchestra. He competed against a lot of great horn players who also wanted that job. Whether or not he thought that he reached peak functioning, the judges on the audition panel thought he played really, really well, or at least better than all the other musicians. In my mind, he executed a flawless performance in the final round to win.

Parker, the golfer who had the new idea for a wedge, needed to prepare for peak functioning as he was getting ready to meet with the staff at Titleist. He had a poster of how they could monetize his revolutionary wedge, what the benefits would be to the company, and how they could customize the design. He was working on his sales pitch from top to bottom.

When he started practicing for me, I suggested places where he could be more confident, or where he could bring up the energy. We fine-tuned the presentation to make it more appealing for the people who would be in the room. Parker recalls, "I needed to be able to problem-solve on the fly. I needed to be able to clear up any doubts that they might have. I had to show them that I had total confidence in what I created. It could significantly change golfers' short game shots by being set up correctly at address with their wedges, hopefully with Titleist wedges with my alignment lines on them."

Parker learned everything he could about the meeting so that he could practice it in his mind over and over. He knew who would be at the meeting and what holes could be poked in his idea. "Don and I talked a lot about imagining the meeting going extremely well, making a great pitch to the staff, and answering all of their questions effectively. I envisioned the desired reality that I intended to create. I visualized myself concluding a very successful pitch and signing a contract with Titleist for my wedges, and then seeing them sold to amateur and professional golfers all over the world."

His preparation became very nitty-gritty, down to the details, so that he could imagine a successful event clearly in his mind. Remember what we discussed in week two about creating successful events? Parker used this practice to enormous advantage. "We went into everything from the clothes that I was going to wear to my body language. Was I going to be standing or sitting? What was I going to do with my hands? All that stuff was very calculated because none of it was normal and natural for me. I'm used to gripping a club and swinging it, not making a business pitch."

Parker had to envision a successful event, because he'd experienced a long period of losing his sense of who he was, and his confidence had suffered. Imagining and visualizing his success helped bring it to reality. "I felt like it took work to raise myself up and get that confidence back. I needed to portray confidence and belief in what I had created. I couldn't come across as the former pro golfer who was just trying to find his way after leaving the tour. I had to come across as the inventor who just came up with the greatest thing since sliced bread."

Practicing for the pitch became a way for Parker to transition out of one identity and enter into another. It was a hero's journey if I've ever seen one. "It's hard to transition out of something that I was so good at for a long time and then to decline and not be as good at it. Now it's like I've got this new identity. I'm not that person anymore. I'm transitioning into being an inventor and somebody who's come up with something that's game-changing and really impactful. It took some work to step into that new role with confidence."

Here are my recommendations for you to do today or during this step:

- Increase your taper
- Practice centering up 6 times
- Drink lots of water to flush out the stress chemicals in your body
- Replace them with happy neurochemicals
- Use the cue utilization strategy throughout the day
- Write all the things that you're grateful for
- Follow your routine in the morning

Remember, your sleep is very important with only days before your big event. You need to get quality sleep, hopefully through the night, with a minimum number of disruptions or their effects. Unfortunately, good rest and sleep can be disturbed by dreams, especially if they are anxiety dreams. They are common, especially in the last few nights before important and consequential events.

Before getting into bed, write down any unresolved things that you need to work on tomorrow on a piece of paper or in your journal or notebook. If you have recurring anxiety dreams, write out better endings for those dreams, and then visualize them. Put certain categories of dreams (your performance, financial issues, relationships, etc.) off-limits for the rest of the night. If you wake up from an unpleasant story or situation, realize that it was just an anxiety dream.

If you need to use the bathroom, plan to find it without exposing your eyes to light. That would give the signal for your brain to wake up. Get back in bed immediately and find a comfortable position. Center and focus on slow, deep breathing while you relax all your muscles. Shut off your brain and go back to sleep. This is not the time for you to do dream analysis. I'll save you the trouble. Anxiety—or any other—dreams that wake you up mean the same thing: that you were sleeping. Go back to sleep as soon as possible. Pleasant dreams.

Week 4

Friday or Step 21

I offer my congratulations to you for making it this far. Your big day is quickly approaching. At this time, you should be feeling like you're sitting on top of a rocket ship that's about to launch. Be grateful for the extra energy. You can use it very soon. In the meantime, record at least seven things in your journal or notebook that you are truly grateful for, as well as thankfulness for achieving peak functioning in your upcoming performance.

Morning Routine:

- ✓ Wake up to energizing music
- ✓ Drink 8 oz water
- ✓ Splash cold water on your face at least 7 times
- ✓ Get outside within minutes
- ✓ Stretch and walk, bike or jog briskly
- ✓ Center after you get home
- ✓ Practice mindfulness for 3 minutes

Increase your taper today. Work even less or not at all on your physical playing or performance. Try not to burn off any of the extra energy that you are feeling. I hope that you had a good night's rest. If not, and if you feel inclined to take a nap, please keep it to 20 minutes in the early afternoon. Before your performance, look over your journal or notebook writings and recall all the exercises that you've completed. Review the topics we've covered.

For the rest of today or during this step, focus on your taper, take it easy, and get more rest and relaxation. Besides going into your upcoming performance event fresh and rested with lots of positive energy, you need to be in a great mood. Continue to maintain your attitude of gratitude. Today is a great time to drink extra water and flood your nervous system with happy neurochemicals.

Here are some ways to keep those happy neurochemicals coming. Dopamine levels will increase in your system today with R&R, a nap, and more quality sleep tonight. Anticipating pleasurable feelings today, like taking a leisurely stroll in nature or getting a massage, will also release dopamine and make you feel better. Being out in the fresh air and sunlight will cause serotonin to enter into your nervous system. That should also put you in a good mood.

Listen to your favorite music or watch comedies that will improve your mood. You can increase oxytocin levels with physical affection, pleasurable activities, and time with close friends and loved ones. If you eat dark chocolate, it will release endorphins into your system, which will also help your emotional state.

One last thing that will keep your mind in a happy state is to smile. Even if you're just faking a smile, the physical act of smiling has the same effect on your brain. It can literally trick your brain into believing that you are happy. Countless scientific studies have proven that smiling relaxes the body and elevates mood states. So, practice your smile today and show your teeth. Find a genuine smile, focus on thankfulness for this coming opportunity to achieve peak functioning.

The Components of Peak Functioning

Now we can synthesize all the common aspects of peak experiences, flow states, the zone, and peak performance into the seven components of peak functioning. This level of superior execution is far beyond the optimal range; it is where truly amazing things can happen. These temporary episodes are beyond our absolute control. But if you use all seven components, you can make them more likely to occur, happen more frequently, and hopefully last longer.

In order to execute at a peak level of functioning, you will need to challenge your highest capabilities to bring out your very best. That's why you will need to commit ahead of time to playing the edge, way beyond your ego's limiting thoughts, beliefs, and irrational fears. Before you begin, make sure that you summon up all of your courage and willpower so you can really go for it, without any regard for the consequences, and let it fly! If you do, you can surely handle whatever happens after that, since you will know that you went for it, which will probably help to produce your best execution ever!

Your level of confidence needs to be sky-high and match or exceed the level of difficulty of the activity that you've chosen. Hopefully, your level of self-trust is at an all-time high, too. However, that doesn't mean it's reached a peak, as of yet. As you know, your level of belief and self-trust is the result of three principal factors: positive self-talk, visualizing your very best execution, taking the correct actions, always striving for excellence, not perfection. Just do your best, no matter what.

Today especially, make sure that you consciously and deliberately form the requisite positive mindset to achieve peak functioning and flawless execution. That means maintaining a very optimistic outlook with an assured attitude of positive expectancy that things are going to go really well in your event. Hold the image of that in your mind with the idea that you are ready to create something truly exceptional in your performance, until you actually create it in reality.

In the meantime, your full-time job today is to convince yourself beyond any doubt whatsoever that you are going to perform your very best tomorrow in the live event. You must fully believe in your greatest capabilities without reservation, qualification, or condition. At this high level of confidence, you can be grateful in advance for your ability to achieve peak functioning and to have a flawless performance.

Greg's final dive in Seoul on the 10-meter offers a wonderful illustration of peak functioning. He recalls this event in his own words:

> After the crowd finally quieted down from the previous diver, I stepped out to the end of the platform, got my toes to the edge of the platform, got my feet set and took a breath. I looked across to the other side of the pool, where the water hits the gutter, to make sure that my head was in line and my posture was correct. I took another breath, and then I went to only one thought—because you can only think of one thing at a time in order to be successful: 'relax your shoulders.' Then I could swing my arms through and allow my body to do what it was trained to do.
>
> I swung my arms up, pulled my knees up and into my chest and squeezed. I could feel the rotation begin. We spot the surface of the water so that we know where we are in relation to where we are in space. I did the first rotation, saw my spot, did the second rotation, got my spot, and then the third rotation, I saw my spot. I saw that I was a little closer to the water and lower than I would have liked to have been, so I knew that I had to kick my legs up, rather than out, in order to wind up vertically and not short of the rotation. A reverse three and a half is so difficult, you don't have a whole lot of time to stretch out and get lined up. You're right on top of it, so it feels like the crash position as your hands hit the water.

I broke the surface with my hands, and as I entered the water, I had to reach back pretty hard to pull my body in line because I was going short of vertical. I heard my hands breaking the surface of the water and then I felt the water rushing against my body. From that point on, I couldn't hear anything except the hum of the water pump. It's a deafening silence that only divers know. Even though I was in a building with thousands of people, I was all by myself for those few moments before I surfaced.

I started swimming to the surface of the water with that question, was it enough? I knew it was good, but was it enough? As my head came out of the water, I could feel the vibration of the applause and the cheering before I heard it, because the water was still draining out of my ears. And then the sound of the crowd was just as amazing. It was also incredibly emotional, because I knew that it was probably my last competitive dive of my life.

I remember popping out of the pool, grabbing my towel and throwing it over my face because I was afraid to see the scoreboard. I was fearful of what I'd see. I was welling up with these emotions. I was holding back the tears because I knew this was probably my last competitive dive, but I didn't want anybody to see me crying because I knew that six months prior to those Olympic games I had been diagnosed HIV positive. This was 1988. And in 1988, if you were diagnosed with HIV, that was a death sentence. I was 28 at the time and I was sure that I would never see my 30th birthday.

I focused on my coach because I couldn't look at the scoreboard. I just could focus on him. He was intensely looking at that scoreboard, and then all of a sudden, I saw the corners of his mouth lift up, and then his smile radiated to his eyes. His son jumped over the partition that was separating us from the rest of the world and gave his father a big hug. They were jumping up and down in celebration, and that's how I knew that I won.

By that time, I couldn't hold the tears back. People thought I was crying because I won. They didn't know that it was the emotional culmination of an incredibly difficult few months and my last competitive dive. It was all over, and we had done it. There was no need to hold anything back now, and I didn't. I couldn't. I just cried and cried. At some point after all the hugging and crying, Ron and I separated. I had to get ready for the awards ceremony. When the ceremony began, Ron was on the deck with [his wife] Mary Jane near the podium. I could tell they were both crying. And of course, I was crying too.

The banquet was very emotional. Each athlete got up to give his or her thanks. When it was my turn, I went up to the podium and thanked all the appropriate people. Then I turned to Ron and said, "Ron, I couldn't have gotten through this without you. It took all ten years of our experience together, and a lot of love and trust to get through a difficult week." I started crying and that was the end of my speech. I simply couldn't say anymore. I left the podium and went to Ron's table, and we hugged and cried. We didn't talk. We just cried.

With all the difficulty that Greg faced that week, he must have witnessed his shadow's looming presence, but it obviously did not prevent his flawless execution under extreme pressure. At some point today, hopefully sooner rather than later, you need to have another session with your dark side. It's important that you understand and resolve any of your dark side's current resentments, not to mention any previous resentments that may still exist. Meet with your shadow again in order to gain your dark side's contribution, or at least its non-resistance to your upcoming event, so that you achieve a peak level of functioning.

"The hero is the one who conquers the dragon, not the one who is devoured. Only one who has risked the fight with the dragon and is not overcome by it wins the hoard, the treasure hard to attain." Carl Jung

Pre-event Shadow Meeting: Session 7

1. Get centered.
2. Become open-minded, compassionate, non-judgmental, tolerant, curious, and friendly, accepting and appreciating your shadow.
3. Sit quietly for at least a minute to clear your mind.
4. See your shadow sitting in front of you. Greet it by name. Express your gratitude to it for communicating with you and continuing to reveal itself to you on a conscious level.
5. Ask your dark side again for its forgiveness for whatever you may have done to it or allowed to happen to it.
6. Ask if there's anything you can do for your shadow. Find out what it may still want but has not gotten yet. Take notes. Suggest how you may be able to remedy the situation.
7. Ask your shadow for its cooperation in your performance. Let it be as a combined and united effort with the singular mission of flawless execution.
8. Negotiate a reward for your shadow's total cooperation, contingent upon your successful performance. Draw up a new contract and sign it.
9. Express your sincere love for your dark side, with all of its imperfections, powerful energy and redeeming qualities.
10. Embrace all of the wonderful and unique aspects of your whole self, as you continue to grow in unity, harmony, and love.

Now it is time to start into your full taper, doing much less and resting much more. You must recover the energy that you have spent over the last few weeks. Where do you get that vital energy? By getting extra sleep and rest in the final part of your taper, as in now. Try to get outside for some fresh air and sunshine. Take a long, leisurely walk-in nature, if possible, by a body of water or in a forest. You need to get happy chemicals in your system so you can be in the right state of mind during the event.

As part of your tapering process, practice mental rehearsal several times today or during this step. You must be able to clearly see yourself executing your best performance in vivid and complete detail. Make sure that you can fully sense the correct movements in your body, and that you can clearly hear the sounds that you intend to create. Get everything right in your body and mind well before you perform.

Deborah found all of this preparation for her dance competition very helpful. About two weeks before her event, she ramped up her mental rehearsal, spending about twenty minutes a day visualizing her moves. The night before the event, she laid out her clothing, shoes, jewelry, and everything she would wear. "Everything is ready so that I don't have to be scrambling around looking for it, creating more tension. Oftentimes, we women have very, very early hair and makeup appointments, like 4:00 am, so that we can get prepared before we get on the floor. So getting everything ready is really important."

She made sure her dance bag was packed, and then she laid out her yoga mat to do some stretching and meditative breathing, using her cue words to get to a quiet mental place. She did a small amount of mental rehearsal. Deborah pulled her journal out before her performance. "I have a dance book that I write positive affirmations in… things that I've read or seen that struck me as really positive or that affected me in a good way. Sometimes I just read through my little book and see some of the things that I found. Sometimes I write out my fears and also their balance with a positive thought."

When Deborah started to get anxious, she remembered why she was doing this:

> It's not just about doing a job, because I think I used to think
> of it as a job, as in, I've got to remember the choreography,

and to connect with my partner, the direction on the floor, like step-by-steps, but the reality is what you really need to remember is, what do I bring to the audience? What can I bring to the judges? Why do I do this? Why does anybody compete over and over and over again? If you're not enjoying it, that's like the burning question all the time is why are you doing this?

What do you want to accomplish? What do you want to show? What is it? You need to show the joy that you feel when you dance. When you're being judged, all of the judges are professional dancers, and they've danced all their lives. It's the thing they love. You should show them that you love it, too, not that you're totally stressed out and freaked out about it.

She realized, too, that it was important to remember all the work she'd done.

You did it, you did the work, now it's time to show it and peak and let all your energy out on the floor and let it flow in a really positive way and make it beautiful. You take that big bubble of anxiety and squish, squish, squish, squish it down until it's manageable, and then you funnel it through this tube where all the excited little neurons are floating around. At the end, you're on the dance floor and all the energy comes out. All the beauty comes out. Your hands are beautiful. Your back is beautiful. Your dress is gorgeous. All the joy is out there. That's my visual of how it happens.

The day before Bart was going to record his audition video, I told him to taper and recover from all the extra practice he had been putting in. That day, he should do nothing in terms of playing his instrument. Bart recalls taking a nice walk, lying in bed, and having a really lazy day so that on Tuesday, the next day, he would be completely fresh and rested.

Bart later said, "Dr. Greene taught me different ways of taking time away from your instrument, so you can conserve your energy in the time leading up to the audition recording. Then you can go into the sessions with the extra energy that you'll need in order to sustain your focus and keep it sharp until you've finished all the recordings and you're satisfied with them." As previously reported, Bart won the audition for the position with the symphony orchestra in Poland.

Parker, too, was ready to face his final challenge. He had a one-page script written out, and he would be meeting with the head of the wedge department, the head engineer, the head of the tour department for wedges, and the head of marketing for wedges. "Thankfully, because they are a golf club manufacturer, I was able to make my sales presentation outside, on their driving range. The engineer looked at one of the clubs and said, 'Oh, that's like a neat training device.' But I knew that they didn't make any kind of training devices or instructional aids; they're into functional golf equipment that works on the golf course. I couldn't have him thinking that this club is just a neat training device."

The thought that it's "just a neat training device" could have been like one of those pins that pops a balloon, but Parker had been training and practicing for this very moment. He recalls:

For me, it was like, 'okay, that pin just went in the balloon, but I need to blow up another balloon and show this guy how this works.' I shifted the conversation back to showing him on the driving range why these alignment lines were not only a functional enhancement, but an absolute necessity. I hit a number of different shots to the nearby green: pitches, chip shots, and bump and runs. Several wound up close to the hole. The engineer said they were good shots because I'd been a tour pro, dismissing how helpful the alignment could be. I needed to prove to him that this was a functional club for daily use on the golf course, especially for shots around the greens.

At Parker's suggestion, the group took a break. Then he passed one of his wedges to the engineer and suggested he take a shot. The engineer replied, "I don't have a very good game." So, Parker put a bunch of balls down and showed him how to put his hands on the club to line up the lines to hit the different shots to the green. He was obviously not a very experienced golfer, and he asked a million questions. I told him that all he had to do was look down and line up the lines correctly by adjusting his hands."

Once he'd figured out how to line up his hands for the different shots, Parker left him alone with a small bucket of balls and told him to have some fun. "When our meeting resumed, he told the rest of the staff that he'd just hit some of the best chips and pitch shots of his life."

In order to get through this meeting, Parker said he "relied a lot on centering, slowing my heart rate down and focusing, and having those tools at my disposal. Not just one tool, but a handful to help with the nervous energy, to ground me and keep me focused on the task at hand. Those types of techniques were essential for when I was playing golf at the highest level, and those same techniques translated to my pitch. It was the same nerves, the same butterflies."

In the end, those techniques were vital to Parker because he had to manage his internal emotions in a new role and the new experience of making a business pitch. He had to remember not to speak too fast, or not to gloss over important items in his presentation. He needed to remember to speak well, smile, and be clear in what he said to the group so that the entire staff would understand and appreciate what he was trying to explain:

> Knowing how to slow it down through the centering process was vitally important to making a great pitch to the staff at Titleist. I told them that I could already imagine players on the PGA tour on TV using my wedge. I could also see the camera zooming with a closeup of the wedge in one of the leader's hands.

And then boom, they hit a great chip or pitch or bunker shot. I could clearly see that in my mind. I'd already envisioned that many times, just like I did with my silver tournament trophy in Reno before actually holding it over my head. But now I was holding a pen, just as I had rehearsed, signing a multi-year exclusive licensing deal with Titleist for my innovative wedge design with the enhanced alignment technology.

The new clubs would be out on the world market within months. That meant that he would be a millionaire again before long. Parker had succeeded in achieving his new goal, even though he had branched out into an area formerly quite unknown to him!

Alexa, too, was moving into a new field with her career in law. It took her quite some time before she received her results from the bar exam, but she passed! She left her former clerking job and moved on to a new law firm where she could practice the kind of law she loved and help people in a meaningful way. I found out, too, that her former coach wanted to refer some clients to me. Evidently, Alexa got a higher score on the bar than any of her previous students.

About a year or so after he won the audition with the Hollywood Bowl Orchestra, Dylan was invited to audition for a one-year position as Associate Principal Horn of the Minnesota Symphony Orchestra. Now, it only took him only three days to get through his shadow work ready to be at his peak level of functioning. He said that this time before his audition, it was much more of a friendly conversation with his shadow and then striking an acceptable deal with his dark side for its cooperation.

Afterwards, he called to say, "I won the audition, but more importantly, I learned about my true wants and desires on a much deeper level. The first time was just brushing the surface and acknowledging the shadow's existence. This time was learning about where my shadow really came from and what it truly wanted. It turns out the shadow is just another part of me and integrating my shadows desires into my life has really opened up another world of possibilities for me."

These are my recommendations for you today or in this step:

- Increase your taper
- Practice centering up 7 times
- Drink lots of water and get happy neurochemicals in your system
- Take a 20-minute power nap in the early afternoon
- Meet with your shadow
- Reach an agreement and sign the document
- Taper for the rest of the day
- Take a long walk, hopefully in nature
- Smile and keep in a good mood
- Get a good night's sleep tonight
- Follow your routine in the morning

Ever since you started your morning routine weeks ago, you have been building your personal power. You did this through a series of correct choices that you made several days a week. Consider all the other things that you've done since you started on this journey to strengthen your volition and willpower. You have hopefully changed a lot of your thoughts and habits, taken full responsibility for your actions and their results, and completed a series of recommended exercises. You took new risks past skepticism, pessimism, and fear. You should now feel a great sense of power and control over your actions.

In order to achieve your highest level of execution, you will go into the performance with unfaltering confidence in your special talents and skills, hero's training, and unique experience. You must believe totally and unconditionally in yourself what you are really capable of doing. At this high level of self-trust, you can be grateful in advance for creating peak functioning in your upcoming performance.

As you know, peak functioning requires total focus in the continuing moment of the here and now exclusively on the task at hand until completed. Before you begin your performance, make sure that you are centered. Switch from left brain beta noise and distraction to right brain quiet, focused in alpha or gamma. Keep your mind in the continuing present moment until you have successfully accomplished your goal.

You have been developing your awareness, attention, and powers of concentration ever since you started practicing centering several weeks ago. You have strengthened your attentional ability. You learned how to focus past your ego's resistance, concentrated in the timeless moment of now, experienced alpha and gamma, and achieved one-pointed concentration in the zone.

When the time finally comes, allow yourself to become totally engaged in the correct execution of your refined skills, absorbed in the real experience, and immersed in a cocoon of concentration. There should be a sense of one-ness between subject and object, or a merging of actor and activity. Try to become totally involved and one with your activity, execution, and your ultimate goal of a flawless performance.

You will need to be in flow to achieve peak functioning. Before you begin, set a clear and challenging goal, as well as your detailed plan for accomplishing it. Commit yourself totally to achieving your intention, no matter what. Make the firm decision to trust your abilities unconditionally when the time comes to go for it.

After you are centered and have started, you will need continuing feedback about how you are doing in the here and now in order to stay in flow. You must remain aware in the present moment that you are on track and executing your skills correctly. Play at the edge of your highest capabilities, where control is possible, but not guaranteed. Be willing to surrender to the experience and let go. You need to get beyond your ego and fears so you can get into flow and let it fly.

In the meantime, drink lots of water, do some light exercise or nothing, and eat healthily. You can spend time watching movies, especially comedies. Laugh out loud. Have a long lunch with a good friend or just sit and listen to your favorite music. Do whatever keeps you in a relaxed state of mind. You don't want to waste energy doing any heavy mental lifting.

Save up that precious energy so that when the time comes tomorrow, you will be able to stay focused until you've completed your performance.

Delay all activities that are not absolutely essential to executing your best at the performance. That includes anything or anyone that consumes your energy, time, or attention. Place yourself off-limits to all outside demands, so you can have more time for yourself.

You may feel guilty for not exercising or practicing the day before the performance, especially when you have extra time. This is the time to do a long mental rehearsal. Imagine yourself being in flow in the zone. Enjoy a book. You could revise your musical playlist. Work at staying passively occupied and mellow today. Take a pleasant trip to one of your favorite areas, watch a stand-up comic, attend a play, or just lay on your couch blissed out. Maintain an attitude of gratitude.

If your performance is in the morning, get up plenty early tomorrow. Move slow, talk slow, eat slow. If your performance is in the afternoon, feel free to sleep in or snooze as long as you'd like. However, regardless of when you get up, you will still need to slow everything down as you go about your morning routine and other activities before the performance.

Try to get to bed tonight around the same time as you did for the last few nights. Follow whatever routine or ways that helped you to go to sleep and get a night of quality sleep. Do not turn on any lights.

If you do not fall asleep after 15 minutes, just lie there and relax. Lying in bed comfortably provides 70% of the value of rest without actually being asleep. So just lie there. Quiet your left-brain thoughts. Imagine sitting by a waterfall, floating on a calm lake looking up at the stars, lying in a hammock swinging gently in a dark room. Or just replay some happy memories. Count your many blessings until you drift off into deep sleep. Shhhhh!

Week 4

Saturday

I hope that you got some good sleep last night. Are you ready? Today you will have another opportunity to execute at your peak level of functioning. After your morning routine, do at least one mental rehearsal session of all the important aspects of your ideal performance. After that, trust yourself, your talent, and your training to courageously go for it and let it fly!

Morning Routine:

✓ Wake up to energizing music

✓ Drink 8 oz water

✓ Splash cold water on your face at least 7 times

✓ Get outside within minutes

✓ Stretch and walk, bike or jog briskly

✓ Center after you get home

✓ Practice mindfulness for 3 minutes

No matter what may have happened during the performance, take a break for at least 15 minutes. Go outside, take a walk or jog, and get some fresh air. Gain some perspective before you evaluate your execution. I can guarantee that it wasn't perfect; it will never be, but I'm sure that there were many excellent moments. When you're ready to evaluate your performance, take out your journal or notebook. Rate your overall performance on a scale from 1 to 99.

Centered _____

Positive mindset _____

Confidence _____

Courage _____

Focus _____

In flow in the zone _____

Whole self _____

Execution _____

Epilogue

A relatively short time ago, when you started on the journey, your performance was likely on a competent level or even better. Since then, you have gone through a number of significant changes, intended to take you to a much higher level, physically, mentally and emotionally. I hope the process caused a major paradigm shift in your mind to a new way of thinking about unforced errors, mistakes, and peak functioning.

Whether you recently executed a flawless performance or not is dependent on what you've done with the information and program that I presented to you. If you only read the text to understand the ideas and see where the journey led, I trust that at least you now understand yourself better. If you tried some of the exercises but not all of them, you've likely progressed, but not as far as you could go. If you selectively adhered to my recommendations, it's no big deal. You can try again if you'd like, now that you know how this system works. It's what you choose to do after that's important.

However, if you followed my recommendations and reached peak functioning, let me be the first to congratulate you on your success. You have reached stage 12 on your hero's journey: Mastery. Welcome you to this very special place. Along the way, you learned about many factors involved in creating flawless execution, especially in consequential performances. For a quick review, here's what we covered on your trek to the peak.

Centering, token economy, learning optimism, left versus right brain, developing a positive mindset, building self-confidence, improving self-talk, using affirmations, mental rehearsal, strengthening courage and willpower, the morning routine, striving for excellence, the importance of laughter and humor, accepting reality, being in the now, judgment versus discernment, creating successful events in reality, the power of imagination, one-pointed concentration, peak experiences, flow states, getting into the zone, self-actualization, the persona and shadow, shadow work, tapering, forgiveness, assimilation and integration into your whole self, death and rebirth, happy neurochemicals, gratitude, and the seven components of peak functioning.

Along the way, you were introduced to many early pioneers of the mind who offered their amazing yet practical wisdom. They included Joseph Campbell, William James, Maxwell Maltz, Sigmund Freud, Abraham Maslow, Carl Jung, and Dr. C. I was very pleased to share some of my most respected clients, coaches, and close friends with you. My sincerest thanks to Coach Craig Poole, Coach Ron O'Brien, Greg, Parker, Alexa, Jacqueline, Deborah, Bart, Katy, Athina, and Dylan.

Now it's time to recover from your expenditure of vital energy. I suggest that you take some time off before starting on your next journey. Yes, there's always another adventure waiting for you. There will be more opportunities to explore even higher realms of your true potential, especially with your shadow's cooperation, hidden talents, and powerful energy.

In the meantime, make sure to reward yourself and your shadow with at least one permanent and symbolic reminder of what you have already accomplished. Share the story of your adventure with the people in your life who you love and those who care about you. Tell them about the hero's journey that led you to loving your whole self with all of your wonderful talents, unique imperfections and unlimited potential to create your best.

List of Works Consulted and Further Reading

The following list is compiled by section and in order of relevance to the text.

Introduction

Campbell, Joseph. *The Hero with a Thousand Faces: The Collected Works of Joseph Campbell.* New York, NY. Pantheon, 1949.

Campbell, Joseph with Moyers, Bill. *The Power of Myth.* New York, NY. Doubletree, 1988.

Campbell, Joseph and Cousineau, Phil (Ed.). *The Hero's Journey: Joseph Campbell on His Life and Work.* New York, NY. Harper Collins, 1990.

Lucas, George. *Star Wars: A New Hope.* Los Angeles, CA. Lucasfilm, 1977.

Week 1

Greene, Donald J. *The Enhancement of the Performance and Judgment of SWAT Officers Involved in Stress-Shooting* (Doctoral Dissertation). San Diego, CA. United States International University, 1984.

Nideffer, Robert M. *Attention Control Training: How to Get Control of Your Mind Through Total Concentration.* New York, Wyden Books, 1978.

Nideffer, Robert M. *Psyched to Win: How to Master Mental Skills to Improve Your Physical Performance.* New York, NY. Leisure Press, 1992.

Ueshiba, Morihei. Translated by Stevens, John. *The Secret Teachings of Aikido*. Tokyo. Kodansha International Ltd., 2007.

Ueshiba, Kisshomaru. *The Spirit of Aikido*. Kodansha International Ltd., 1981.

Westbrook, A. and Ratti, O. *Aikido: The Dynamic Sphere*. Rutland, VT. Charles E. Tuttle Company, 1970.

Hicks, Esther and Jerry. *The Amazing Power of Deliberate Intent: Living the Art of Allowing*. Carlsbad, CA, 2006.

Pink, Daniel H. *A Whole New Mind: Why Right-Brainers Will Rule the Future*. New York, NY. Riverhead Books, 2005.

Blakeslee, T.R. *The Right Brain: A New Understanding of the Mind and Its Creative Powers*. New York, NY. Anchor Press, 1980.

Beilock, Sian. *Choke: What the Secrets of the Brain Reveal About Getting It Right When*

You Have To. New York, NY. Simon & Schuster, 2010.

Stephens, Ransom. *The Left Brain Speaks, The Right Brain Laughs*. Jersey City, NJ. Cleis Press, 2016.

Aylon, Teodoro and Azrin, Nathan. *The Token Economy: A Motivational System for Therapy and Rehabilitation*. New York, NY. Appleton-Century-Crofts, 1968.

Hoover, J. and Aylon, Teodoro. *How to Use Token Economy and Point Systems: How to Manage Behavior, 2nd Edition*. Austin, TX. Pro-Ed Publishing, 1999.

Kazdin, Alan E. *The Token Economy: A Review and Evaluation (The Plenum Behavior Therapy Series*. New York, NY. Springer-Verlag, Inc., 1977.

Covey, Stephen R. *The 7 Habits of Highly Effective People: Powerful Lessons in Personal Change*. New York, NY. Simon & Schuster, 1989.

Clear, James. *Atomic Habits: An Easy and Proven Way to Build Good Habits and Break Bad Ones*. New York, Avery, 2018.

Sterner, Thomas M. T*he Practicing Mind: Developing Focus and Discipline in Your LIfe*. Novato, CA. New World Library, 2005.

Dyer, Wayne. *Being in Balance, 9 Principles for Creating Habits to Match Your Desires*. Carlsbad CA. Hay House, 2006.

Walsch, Neale Donald. *When Everything Changes, Change Everything: In a Time of Turmoil and Path to Peace*. Ashland, OR. Em Nin Books, 2010.

Hendricks, Gay. *The Big Leap: Conquer Your Fear and Take Life to the Next Level*. New York, HarperCollins Publishers, 2009.

Maltz, Maxwell. *Psycho-cybernetics: Tap into the Power of the Subconscious Mind*, New York, NY. Simon and Schuster, 1960.

Seligman, Martin. *Learned Optimism: How to Change Your Mind and Your Life*. New York, NY. Vintage Books, 1990.

Dyer, Wayne W. *You'll See it When You Believe it: The Way to Your Personal Transformation*. New York, NY. William Morrow and Company, Inc., 1989.

Lipton, Bruce H. *The Biology of Belief: Unleashing the Power of Consciousness, Matter, and Miracles*. Carlsbad, CA. Hay House, 2002.

Feltz, Deborah. *Self-Confidence and Sports Performance*. Exercise and Sport Science Reviews, 16, 423- 457, 1988.

Donnelly, Darrin. *Relentless Optimism: How a Commitment to Positive Thinking Changes Everything*. New York, NY. Shamrock Media, Inc., 2017.

Druckman, Daniel and Bjork, Robert A., Eds., *In the Mind's Eye: Enhancing Human Performance*. Washington, D.C., National Academy Press, 1991.

Hofstadter, Douglas R. and Dennett, Daniel. *The Mind's I: Fantasies and Reflections on Self and Soul*. Toronto: Bantam Books, 1981.

Kendall, G., Hrycaiko, D., Martin, G. L., & Kendall, T. The effects of imagery, relaxation, and self-talk package on basketball game performance. *Journal of Sport and Exercise Physiology*, 12, 157- 166.

Noel, R.C. The effect of visuomotor behavior rehearsal on tennis performance. *Journal of Sport Psychology*, 2, 221 – 226.

Feltz, D. L. and Landers, D.M. The effects of mental practice on motor skill learning and performance: a meta-analysis. *Journal of Sport Psychology*, 5, 25-57.

Hall, C. R. Individual differences in the mental practice and imagery of motor skill performance. *Canadian Journal of Applied Sport Science*, 10, 175 – 215.

Louganis, G. *Breaking the Surface: Greg Louganis with Eric Marcus*. New York, NY, Random House, 1995.

Jeffers, Susan. *Feel the Fear and Do It Anyway: Dynamic Techniques for Turning Fear, Indecision, and Anger into Power, Action, and Love*. New York, NY. Ballantine Books, 1987.

Murphy, Michael. *Golf in the Kingdom*. New York, NY. Penguin Books, 1972.

Greene, Donald J. *Fight Your Fear and Win: 7 Skills for Performing Your Best Under Pressure - at Work, in Sports, on Stage*. New York, NY. Broadway Books, 2001.

Jampolsky, Gerald G. *Love Is Letting Go of Fear*. Millbrae, CA. Celestial Arts, 1979.

Week 2

Maltz, Maxwell and Kennedy, Dan. *The New Psycho-cybernetics; The Original Science of Self- Improvement and Success That Has Changed the Lives of 30 Million People*. New York, NY. Prentice Hall, 2002.

Elrod, Hal. *The Miracle Morning: The Not-So Obvious Secret Guaranteed to Transform Your Life Before 8 AM*. Hal Elrod International, 2017.

Goleman, Daniel. *Focus: The Hidden Driver of Excellence.* New York, NY. HarperCollins Publishers, 2013.

Herrigel, Eugen. Translated by Hull, R.F. *The Method of Zen.* New York, NY. Pantheon Books, 1960.

Watts, Alan. *The Way of Zen.* New York, NY. Pantheon Books, 1957.

Newport, Cal. *Deep Work: Rules for Focused Success in a Distracted World.* New York, NY. Grand Central Publishing, 2016.

Hewitt, David. Focus: *Best Ways to Improve Your Concentration and Improve Your Learning.* London, Lulu, 2015.

Mack, Gary. *Mind Gym: An Athlete's Guide to Inner Excellence.* New York, NY. McGraw Hill, 2001.

Smith, Ann W. *Overcoming Perfectionism: Finding the Key to Balance and Self-Acceptance.* Deerfield Beach, FL. Health Communications, Inc., 2013.

Ben-Shahar, Tal. *The Pursuit of Perfect: How to Stop Chasing Perfection and Start Living a Richer and Happier Life.* New York, NY. McGraw Hill, 2009.

Martin, Sharon C. *The CBT Workbook for Perfectionism: Evidence-Based Skills to Help You Let Go of Self-Criticism, Build Self-Esteem, and Find Balance.* Oakland, CA. New Harbinger Publications, 2019.

Szymanski, Jeff. *The Perfectionist's Handbook: Take Risks, Invite Criticism, and Make the Mistakes.* Hoboken, NJ. John Wiley & Sons, 2011.

Sachs, Michael L.; Tashman, Lauren S., and Razon, Selen (Eds.). *Performance Excellence: Stories of Success from the Real World of Sport and Exercise Physiology.* New York, NY. Rowman and Littlefield, 2020.

Orlick, Terry. In *Pursuit of Excellence: How to Win in Sports and Life Through Mental Training.* Champaign, IL. Human Kinetics Publishers, 1980.

Ericsson, Anders K. (Ed.) *The Road to Excellence: The Acquisition of Expert Performance in the Arts, Sciences, Sports and Games.* Mahway, NJ. Lawrence Erlbaum Associates, Inc. Publishers, 1996.

Dahlkoetter, Jo Ann. *Your Performing Edge: The Complete Mind-Body Guide to Excellence in Sports, Health, and Life.* San Carlos, CA. Pulgas Ridge Press, 2002.

Leith, Larry M. *The Psychology of Achieving Sports Excellence: A Self-Help Guide for All Athletes.* Toronto, ON. Sports Books Publishers, 2008.

Ravizza, Ken and Hanson, Tom. *Heads Up Baseball: Playing the Game One Pitch at a Time.* Tampa, FL. Hanson House, 2016.

Morgan, W.P. Mind over matter. In W.F. Straub & J.M. Williams (Eds.), *Cognitive Sport Psychology.* Lansing, NY. Sports Sciences International, 1984.

Dychtwald, Ken. *Body-Mind: A Breakthrough Approach to the Secrets of Self-Awareness.* New York, NY. Jove Publications, Inc., 1978.

Dorfman, Harvey A. *The Mental Game of Baseball: A Guide to Peak Performance.* Lanham, MD. Rowman and Littlefield Publishing Group, 2016.

Garfield, Charles and Bennett, Hal. *Peak Performance: Mental Training Techniques of the World's Greatest Athletes.* Los Angeles. J.P. Tarcher, 1985.

Bornstein, Jeremy. *Annotated Bibliography of Peak Experience, Flow, and Peak Performance.* Pleasant Hill, CA. John F. Kennedy Graduate School of Professional Psychology, 1995.

Stulberg, Brad and Magness, Steve. *Peak Performance: Elevate Your Game, Avoid Burnout, and Thrive with the New Science of Success.* New York, NY. Rodale, 2017.

Gauron, E.F. *Mental Training for Peak Performance.* Lansing, NY. *Sports Science Associates, 1984.*

Mahoney, M.J., Gabriel, T.J., & Perkins, T.S. *Psychological Skills and Exceptional Athletic Performance.* The Sport Psychologist, 1, 1987.

Cousins, Norman. *Anatomy of an Illness as Perceived by the Patient: Reflections on Healing and Regeneration.* New York, NY. W.W. Norton & Company, 1979.

Kataria, Madan. *Laughter Yoga: Daily Laughter Practices for Health and Happiness.* New York, NY. Penguin Books, 2018.

Thorndike, Edward. *The Elements of Psychology.* New York, NY. The Mason Henry Press, 1905.

James, William. Principles of Psychology, New York, NY. Henry Holt, 1890.

Freud, Sigmund. *The Ego and the Id.* New York, NY. W.W. Norton and Company, 1960.

Freud, Sigmund. *The Basic Writings of Sigmund Freud.* New York, NY. Random House, 1995.

Huxley, Aldous. *The Doors of Perception.* New York, NY. Harper and Row, Publishers, 1954.

Smith, Adam. *Powers of Mind.* New York, NY. Ballantine Books, 1979.

Hampden-Turner, Charles. *Maps of the Mind: Charts and Concepts of the Mind and Its Labyrinths.* New York, NY. Macmillan Publishing Company, 1981.

Stern, Jess. *The Power of Alpha Thinking: Miracle of the Mind.* New York, Penguin Books, 1977.Holmes, Ernest. T*he Science of Mind: A Philosophy, A Faith, A Way of Life.* New York, NY. Penguin Putnam, Inc., 1938.

The Standard Edition of the Complete Psychological Works of Sigmund Freud, London. Hogarth Press, 1966.

Gallwey, Tim. *The Inner Game of Tennis.* New York, NY. Random House, 1974.

Gardner, Howard. *The Mind's New Science*. New York, NY. Basic Books, 1988.

Dweck, Carol S. *Mindset: The New Psychology of Success*. New York, NY. Ballantine Books, 2006.

Tolle, Eckhardt. *The Power of Now: A Guide to Spiritual Enlightenment*. Vancouver, B.C., Canada, Namaste Publishing, 1999.

Church, Dawson. *Mind to Matter: The Astonishing Science of How Your Brain Creates Material Reality*. Carlsbad, CA. Hay House, 2018.

DeCharms, R. *Personal Causation*. New York, NY. Academic Press, 1968.

Dyer, Wayne W. *Real Magic: Creating Miracles in Everyday Life*. New York, NY. HarperCollins Publishers, 1992.

McGonigal, Kelly. *The Willpower Instinct: How Self-Control Works, Why It Matters, and What You Can Do To Get More Of It*. New York: The Penguin Group, 2012.

Greene, Don. *Performance Success: Performing Your Best Under Pressure*. New York, NY. Routledge Books, 2002.

Fabritius, Friederike and Hageman, Hans H. *The Leading Brain: Powerful Science-Based Strategies for Achieving Peak Performance*. New York, NY. Penguin Random House, 2017.

Maslow, Abraham. *Toward a Psychology of Being: Maslow's Attempt to Construct a Comprehensive, Systematic and Empirically Based General Psychology and Philosophy*. New York, NY. John Wiley and Sons, 1968.

Maslow, Abraham. *Religions, Values, and Peak-Experiences*. New York, NY. Penguin Books, 1970.

Maslow, Abraham. *The Farther Reaches of Human Nature*. New York, NY. Penguin Books, 1971.

Mittleman, W. Maslow's *Study of Self-Actualization: A Reinterpretation. Journal of Humanistic Psychology*, 31 (1), 114-135, 1991.

Csikszentmihalyi, Mihaly. *Flow: The Psychology of Optimal Experience*. New York, NY. Harper & Row Publishers, 1990.

Csikszentmihalyi, Mihaly. *Beyond Boredom and Anxiety*. San Francisco, CA. Jossey-Bass, 1975.

Stein, G.L, Kimiecik, J.C., Daniels, R.J. & Jackson, S.A. *Psychological Antecedents of Flow*. Personality and Social. Psychology Bulletin, 21 (2), 125-135, 1995.

Jackson, Susan A. & *Csikszentmihalyi, Mihaly. Beyond Boredom and Anxiety. San Francisco, CA. Jossey- Bass, 1975.*

Csikszentmihalyi, Mihaly and Smith-Smith B (ed.). *The Concept of Flow in Play and Learning*. New York, NY. Gardner Press, 1979.

Mihaly. *Flow in Sports: The Keys to Optimal Experiences and Performances*. Champaign, IL. Human Kinetics Publishers, 1999.

Shainberg, L. *Finding the Zone*. New York, NY. The New York Times Magazine, pp 34-39, April, 1989.

Murphy, Shane. *The Achievement Zone: An Eight-step Guide to Peak Performance*. New York, NY. Putnam, 1996.

Porter, Kay. *The Mental Athlete: Inner Training for Peak Performance for All Sports*. New York: William C. Brown and Ballantine Books, 2004.

Nideffer, Robert M. *The Inner Athlete: Mind Plus Muscle for Winning*, Los Gatos, CA, Enhanced Performance Services, 1976.

Ravizza, Ken. *Qualities of the Peak Experience in Sport*. In Silva, J. & Weinberg, R. (Eds.), Psychological Foundations for Sport. Champaign, IL: Human Kinetics Publishers, 1984.

Stulberg, Brad and Magness, Steve. *Peak Performance: Elevate Your Game, Avoid Burnout, and Thrive with the New Science of Success*. New York, NY. Rodale Press, 2017.

Mumford, George. *The Mindful Athlete: Secrets to Pure Performance*. Berkeley, CA. Parallax Press, 2016.

Week 3

Jacobi, Jolande and Hull, R.F.C. (Eds). *C.G. Jung: Psychological Reflections: A New Anthology of His Writings.* Princeton NJ. Bollinger Foundation. 1953.

Jung, Carl G. *The Archetypes and the Collective Unconscious: Collected Works of C.G. Jung.* London. Paidos, 1995.

Jung Carl G. *Man and His Symbols: Conceived and Edited by Carl G. Jung.* London. Paidos, 1985.

Jung, Carl G. *The Relations Between the Ego and the Unconscious,* London. Paidos, 2009.

Jung, Carl G. *The Red Book.* London, Paidos, 2010.

Joel, Billy. *The Stranger.* New York, NY. Columbia Records, CD. 1977.

Camus, Albert. *L'Etranger: The Stranger),* Translated by Ward, Matthew. Paris, France. Gallimard, 1942.

Zweig, Connie and Abrams, Jeremiah (Eds.). *Meeting the Shadow: The Hidden Power of the Dark Side of Human Nature.* New York, NY. Penguin Group, 1979.

Chopra, Deepak; Ford, Debbie; and Williamson, Marianne. *The Shadow Effect: Illuminating the Hidden Power of Your True Self.* New York, NY. HarperCollins Publishers, 2011.

Johnson, Robert A. *Owning Your Own Shadow: Understanding the Dark Side of the Psyche,* New York, NY. Harper Collins, 1993.

Bly, Robert. Booth, William (Ed.) *A Little Book on the Human Shadow,* New York, Harper Collins, 1988.

James B. Maas. *Power Sleep: The Revolutionary Program That Prepares Your Mind for Peak Performance.* New York, NY. HarperCollins Publishers, 2008.

James B. Maas and Davis, Haley. *Sleep To Win: Secrets to Unleash Your Athletic Excellence in Every Sport.* Bloomington, IN. Author House, 2014.

Milner, C. E., & Cote, K. A. (2009). Benefits of napping in healthy adults: Impact of nap length, time of day, age, and experience with napping. *Journal of Sleep Research*, 18, 272 – 281.

Mednick, S. with Ehrman, E. *Take a Nap! Change Your Life: The Scientific Plan to Make You Smarter, Healthier, More Productive:* York, NY. Workman Publishing, 2006.

Afremow, Jim. *The Champion's Mind: How Great Athletes Think, Train, and Thrive.* New York, NY. Rodale Books, 2013.

Loehr, James and Schwartz, Tony, *The Power of Full Engagement: Managing Energy, Not Time, Is the Key to High Performance and Personal Renewal.* New York, NY. Simon and Schuster, 2003.

Berman, Marc C., Jonides, John, and Kaplan, Stephen. *The Cognitive Benefits of Interacting with Nature.* Psychological Sciences Journal, 2008 December; 19 (12): 1207-12.

Craig, Jeffrey and Prescott, Susan L. *Here's Why a Walk in the Woods or a Dip in the Ocean is So Good for Your Health.* The Conversation, University of Western Australia, February, 2016.

Nettle, Daniel. *Happiness: The Science Behind Your Smile.* New York, NY. Oxford University Press, 2005.

Masters, Robert A. *Bringing Your Shadow Out of the Dark: Breaking Free from the Hidden Forces that Drive You.* Boulder, CO. Sounds True, 2018.

Week 4

Perry, Bruce D., M.D., Ph.D. and Winfrey, Oprah. *What Happened to You? Conversations on Trauma, Resilience, and Healing,* New York, NY. Flatiron Books, 2021.

Ford, Debbie. *The Dark Side of the Light Chasers: Reclaiming Your Power, Creativity, Brilliance, and Dreams,* New York, NY. Riverhead Books, 1998.

Cohen, Alan. *The Dragon Doesn't Live Here Anymore: Loving Fully, Living Freely.* Des Moines, WA. Alan Cohen Publications, 1981.

Brown, Brene. *The Gifts of Imperfection: Let Go of Who You Think You're Supposed to Be and Embrace Who You Are.* Center City, MN. Hazelden Publishing, 2010.

Richo, David. Shadow Dance: *Liberating the Power and Creativity of Your Dark Side.* Boston, MA. Shambala Publications, Inc., 1999.

Enright, Robert D., Ph.D. *Forgiveness is a Choice: A Step-by-Step Process for Resolving Anger and Restoring Hope.* Washington D.C.,The American Psychological Association

Dyer, Wayne. *The Awakened Life: Beyond Success, Achievement, and Performance.* New York, NY. Simon & Schuster Audio/Nightingale-Conant, 2006.

Moody, Raymond. *Life After Life: The Investigation of a Phenomenon - Survival of Bodily Death.* New York, NY. Harper One, 1975.

Lommel, Pim. *Consciousness Beyond Life*: *The Science of the Near-Death Experience.* New York, NY. Harper One, 2007.

Long, Jeffrey. Evidence of the Afterlife: *The Science of Near-Death Experiences.* New York, NY. Harper Collins, 2010.

Zeigarnik, Bluma. *On Finished and Unfinished Tasks.* In A Sourcebook of Gestalt Psychology, ed. Ellis, W.D. London. Kegan, Paul, Trench, and Company, 1938.

Coles, Nicholas and Larsen, Jeff. *A Meta-analysis of the Facial Feedback Literature: Effects of Facial Feedback on Emotional Experience.* Psychological Bulletin, 2019.

Mazur, Elena. *The Zeigarnik effect and the concept of unfinished business. British Gestalt Journal*, Vol. 5, 1996.

Breuning, Loretta. *Habits of a Happy Brain: Retrain Your Brain to Boost Your Serotonin, Dopamine, Oxytocin, and Endorphin Levels.* Avon, MA. Adams Media, 2016.

Burnett, Dean. *The Happy Brain: The Science of Where Happiness Comes from and Why.* New York, NY. W.W. Norton & Sons, 2018.

Emmons, R. A., & McCullough, M. E. (2004). The Psychology of Gratitude (Series in Affective Science). New York: Oxford University Press.

Emmons, R. A., & Mishra, A. (2011). Why gratitude enhances well-being: What we know, what we need to know. In K. M. Sheldon, T. B. Kashdan, & M. F. Steger (Eds.)

Ryan, J. *Attitudes of Gratitudes: How to Give and Receive Joy Every Day of Your Life.* Newburyport, MA. Coroni Press, 2017.

Sansone, R.A. & Sansone, L.A. (2010). Gratitude and well-being: The benefits of appreciation. Psychiatry (Edgemont), 7(11), p. 18-22.

Lambert, N.M., Graham, S.M., Fincham, F.D., & Stillman, T.F. (2009 November). A changed perspective: How gratitude can affect your sense of coherence through positive reframing. The *Journal of Positive Psychology, 4*(6), p. 461-470.

Duckworth, Angela. *Grit: The Power of Passion and Perseverance.* New York, NY. Scribner, 2016.

Ericsson, Anders K. Hoffman, Robert R., Kozbelt, Aaron, and Wiliams, Mark A. (Eds.). *The Cambridge Book of Expertise and Expert Performance,* 2nd Ed. New York, NY. Cambridge University Press, 2018.

Leonard, George. *Mastery: The Keys to Long Term Success and Fulfillment.* New York, NY. Penguin Group, 1991.

Acknowledgements

$\mathcal{F}$irst of all, I want to offer my heartfelt love and appreciation to my mom, dad, Uncle Joe, Len, and Aunt Dot for their loving guidance from the earliest moments and throughout my life. As a young athlete, I was also fortunate to have three great coaches: Freddy Hashagen in gymnastics and trampoline, Tom Boris in butterfly and water polo, and John Barroncini in springboard and platform diving.

Thanks to several upperclassmen at West Point, Wayne Schaltenbrand, Kerry O'Hara, and Ken Cummings, who all taught me how to successfully navigate the military academy. I am also forever grateful to my profound mentors in grad school. These world-renowned sports psychologists, Dr. Bruce Ogilvie, Dr. Robert Nideffer, and Dr. Christina Ferrera, introduced me to their specialties and expertise counseling professional and Olympic athletes.

I am so fortunate to have known a number of experienced Olympic coaches from whom I learned about the highest levels of competition. A special thanks goes to Ron O'Brien, Larry Liebowitz, Terry Stoddard, Mark Schubert, Nort Thornton, Julian Krug, Matt Scoggin, Tim O'Brien, Richard Quick, Jack Nelson, Craig Poole, Al Joyner, and Art Venegas. They taught me how to train athletes to win Olympic medals in diving, swimming and track and field.

I came to understand the mindset of professional golfers by working alongside several top golf instructors at Golf Digest Schools. My sincere appreciation goes to such legends as Davis Love, Jr., Bob Toski, Paul Runyan, DeDe Owens, Hank Johnson, Chuck Cook, and Peter Kostis. Thanks to Skip Barber and his awesome teachers, as well as

Steve Shelton and Nick Ham, for sharing their knowledge of Grand Prix racing with me.

Although I was new to classical music after leaving golf and motor racing, I was warmly welcomed by President Joseph Polisi and Michael Tillson Thomas, the Director of the New World Symphony Orchestral Academy. As a result, I was able to spend quality time with some of their finest teachers: Dorothy DeLay, Itzhak Perlman, Joe Alessi, Elaine Douvas, Heidi Castleman, Jeanne Baxstresser, Daniel Cataneo, Carol Wincenc, and Julie Landsman.

Since then, I was also fortunate to learn from other master teachers in various performing arts disciplines. These mentors include Gail Williams, Frank Almond, Ted Adkatz, Floyd Cooley, Warren Deck, David Geber, Margaret Osborne, Samatha Graham, Lynn Quo, Sycil Mathai, Joe Illick, Sean Reusch, Sharon Daniels, Kenny DiCarlo, Lynn Aspnes, Maitland Peters, Laura Greenwald, Pat Nott, Michael Linville, Keith Buhl, Tom Sherwood, James Fayette and Jennifer Ringer.

Along the way, I have been blessed with many wonderful friends. These fine folks include Louis Velasquez, Judy Zunamon Lewis, Doug Hall, Bobby Garcia, Nancy Millstein, Maureen McCormick, Vernon Buchman, Jimmy Freese, Dr. Ben Lisch, Milan Milosivich, Charles Pilon, Sheldon Person, Tom and Karen Kamp, Dr. Alexander Hopster, Michele Wrighte, Jimmy Freese and Eleanor Weingartner.

Even before I began writing, I relied heavily upon two very talented women. Without these ladies, this work would never have reached completion. International best-selling author, Kathy Rose, read every word of each version of the text and always offered the most incredible but wise and supportive feedback. Erin Armstrong also contributed crucial, well thought out ideas, much-needed edits, and encouragement throughout the process. I can't thank you enough for your patience and brilliance. Thank you so much to John for sharing valuable time with his talented wife, and to Nora and Breen, for sharing their precious mom with me.

I want to credit Alan Hebel and Ian Koviak for their wonderful work on the cover design. Thanks to Emily Mace, Kimi Dohi, Sarah Krueger and Olivier Kastel for their help with the editing, illustrations, and diagrams. Merci beaucoup to Aurelien Chaudagne for his assistance with the computer work and technical details on the backend of my websites.

A special thanks goes out to my awesome publishing and marketing team at Hasmark Publishing International in Toronto. They include CEO and President, Judy O'Beirn and her impressive staff including Jenna Ventura, Niki Rowland, Monika Skrobek, Mary-Kate Luke, Kelly Vurinaris, Talita Pereira, Jenn Gibson, Alison Malcolm, Ashley Constant, Michaela Pitman, and Amit Dey.

I'm so indebted to those individuals who allowed me to share their struggles with the hero's journeys with you. Thank you so much to Greg, Parker, Athina, Bart, Deborah, Alexa, Dylan, Jacky, Jason, and Katy. I'm sure that many folks will profit from your stories. Without formal recognition, I also want to express my gratitude to all my former students and clients for sharing important parts of your lives and careers with me. I trust that you're doing well.

As I'm moving on to my next project, I'd like to acknowledge two of my well-trained proteges. Richard Mann served in the Special Forces in the United Kingdom. He is a master of all the sports psychology strategies and exercises that are presented in this text. Richard trains professional boxers, Brazilian jiu-jitsu fighters and premiere football (soccer) teams to achieve their full potential under pressure. You can contact him in London at ManOnAMission.com

Award winning violinist Gabriela Piexoto lives in Portugal. She teaches violin and piano at the Academy of Music in Viana do Castelo and the Conservatory of Music in Barcelos. She is a master of the methods for helping all types of performing artists achieve peak functioning and flawless execution under high stress. Gabriela is currently finishing a book on the subject. You can also watch her on YouTube at https://www.youtube.com/watch?v=_hMjZ0Jeyrg]

Finally, and most importantly, I would like to express my deepest gratitude to my highly respected colleague and close friend, Annie Bosler, DMA. I've been so fortunate to have her amazing help and guidance in my career over the last several years. If I have reached any degree of success since we met years ago, it's largely due to her involvement. My words cannot fully express my appreciation for this special woman in my life, but I'll try.

Annie is one of the most impressive but understated individuals I've ever known. She was a double major at Carnegie Mellon in both classical music (French horn) and math, and also played on the school's tennis team. She eventually became a sought-after studio musician in LA, teacher, professor, and mentor to many fortunate students and players throughout southern California. Annie is also an author, documentary producer and Ted-Ed contributor.

She is extremely dedicated to her family and students, but she shared a huge amount of her precious time, energy, and sweet caring to me in my life. Her son, Henry is less than 3, but thanks to his dad Dylan, he can already hit a scaled down driver into or over a net in their backyard. It really helps to have loving parents who are also great teachers and performers.

About the Author

*D*on Greene graduated from the US Military Academy at West Point. After paratrooper and commando training, he was the first in his class to join the Army's Special Forces (Green Berets). In 1984, Dr. Greene became the sports psychologist for the US Olympic Diving Team. Following the '88 Olympics, he worked with Division I football teams (Stanford, Texas, Minnesota) and individual pro athletes and teams (Grand Prix champions, Texas Rangers).

In 1994, Dr. Greene began working with auditioning musicians. After several of his clients won major auditions (the Houston Symphony, the Chicago Lyric Opera, and the Met Orchestra), he was invited to be on the faculty of The Juilliard School, where he taught for many years. In 2017, he was named a TED Educator and produced, *How to practice effectively…for just about anything*. This video immediately went viral, ultimately receiving over 30 million views.

During the recent pandemic, Dr. Greene mentored athletes, performers, creative artists and business execs on Zoom and Skype. He wrote a monthly column for the NY Musician's Union on ways to deal with the incredible chaos, extra stress, and uncertainty about the future. Before, during, and after the pandemic he wrote *Train Your Own Hero*. Three years in the making, he is now delighted to be able to share this with you and hopes that it helps you achieve happiness with your highest level of functioning.

Book Page

Books and more by Don Greene, Ph.D.

The Enhancement of the Performance and Judgement of SWAT Officers Involved in Stress Shooting

Audition Success: An Olympic Sports Psychologist Teaches Performing Artists How to Win

Performance Success: Performing Your Best Under Pressure

Fight Your Fear and Win: 7 Skills for Performing Your Best Under Pressure at Work, in Sports, on Stage

Score Your Best on Tests: Train Your Mind like an Olympic Champion for Standardized Exams

College Prep for Musicians: A Comprehensive Guide for Students, Parents, Teachers, and Counselors. Co-authored with Annie Bosler, D.M.A. and Kathleen Tesar, Ed.D.

How to Practice Effectively…For Just About Anything. Ted-Ed Presentation with Dr. Annie Bosler

Sales Page

Dr. Don Greene's services, books, products and contact information are available through his websites. Services include one-on-one sessions with Dr. Greene via Skype, Zoom, phone, or in person at his office in Pasadena, CA, and speaking engagements with athletic teams, performing arts conferences, wellness programs, and workshops.

Dr. Greene has created several assessments to identify individual strengths and specific areas of improvement for different types of performances or activities. These assessments and their targets are as follows. A performance mastery assessment for musicians, dancers, actors, singers, and public speakers. An exam skills assessment for students taking standardized exams. The fight your fear and win assessment is for performers and business executives. The learning styles and competitive styles assessments are for amateur and professional athletes. The individual player and team assessments are for esport gamers. The teaching styles assessment is for athletic coaches and performing arts teachers.

Dr. Greene offers several online, self-study courses, which you can complete at your own pace. They all include an accompanying workbook and videos. The courses are: a performance mastery course, which includes the performance mastery assessment; Power Learning: The Ultimate Guide to Better Practice Habits; and the Centering Training Course, for athletes, performing artists, standardized test takers, and business executives. These are all available through the websites:

www.WinningOnStage.com
www.WinningInSports.com

HEARTS to be HEARD

Giving a Voice to Creativity!

With every donation, a voice will be given to
the creativity that lies within the hearts of
our children living with diverse challenges.

By making this difference, children that may
not have been given the opportunity to have their
Heart Heard will have the freedom to create
beautiful works of art and musical creations.

Donate by visiting

HeartstobeHeard.com

We thank you.

CPSIA information can be obtained
at www.ICGtesting.com
Printed in the USA
BVHW041342111022
649148BV00019B/1181/J